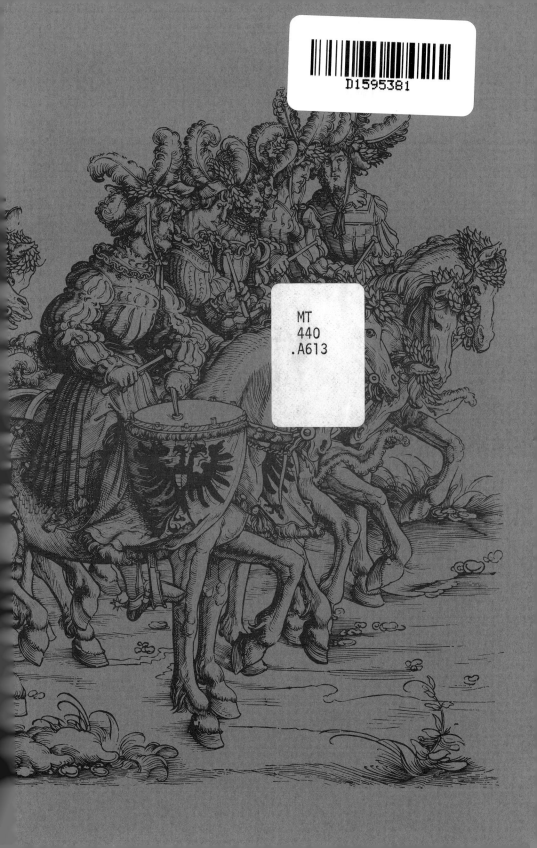

Announcement

A certain author, who at this time does not yet wish to be named, but who is—as far as we know—a trained trumpeter who has served in this quality for many years at a princely court in Germany, is now publishing a work with the title: *The Court and Field Trumpeters' and Military Kettledrummers' Heroic and Musical Art (Die heroisch-musikalische Hof- und Feld-Trompeter- und Heerpauckerkunst).* We have had the opportunity to look through the work in manuscript and [we] believe that the author's efforts will not be for naught, all the more so as [the work] helps to fulfill [our] wish for a proper and complete method *(Lehrbuch)* for every common modern musical instrument. To be sure, it is not a matter for everyone to [wish to] play the trumpet or to occupy himself with beating the kettledrum; but it can easily be proper for every music lover and valuable for every professional musician, especially composers, to have some knowledge of these arts. Moreover, many good historical detaiis are gathered together in this work. We wish to include the table of contents here, in order that everyone may be able to judge the work's subject matter for himself.

Subscriptions to this work in the amount of 16 groschen, without any further obligation of payment, will be accepted; when finished, the work will not be sold for less than 1 Imperial thaler. Whoever takes 5 copies together [may] have them for 1 Dutch ducat of full weight. We have not been informed as to the date of publication or the duration of subscription. However, as far as [the date of publication] or the subscription itself are concerned, one has only to apply to **Mr. Johann Ernst Altenburg,** organist in Bitterfeld.

—from *Musikalische Nachrichten und Anmerkungen*, December 10, 1770

As early as December 10, 1770, J. A. Hiller announced in his *Musikalische Nachrichten und Anmerkungen* that he had seen the treatise in manuscript, and that it was being offered on a subscription basis prior to publication. It is interesting to see how Altenburg's book changed its shape between 1770 and 1795—although, of course, it was finished as a whole already then—and in particular to see that Altenburg dropped his idea of an appendix containing a dialogue between a teacher and his pupil. Needless to say, we are all the more grateful to him for his musical appendix containing the concerto. Furthermore, we may suspect that the dialogue found its way into the main text, since there is a lot of material in the printed edition of 1795 devoted to the Imperial Privileges.—E. H. T.

Muſikaliſche

Nachrichten und Anmerkungen.

Ein und funfzigſtes Stück.

Leipzig, den 10ten December 1770.

Nachricht.

Ein gewiſſer Verfaſſer, der zur Zeit noch nicht genannt ſeyn will, ſoviel wir aber wiſſen, ein gelernter Trompeter iſt, und als ſolcher an einem fürſtlichen Hofe in Deutſchland lange Jahre in Dienſten geſtanden hat, läßt jetzt ein Werk drucken, unter dem Titel: Die heroiſch-muſikaliſche Hof- und Feld-Trompeter- und Heerpauckerkunſt. Wir haben Gelegenheit gehabt, das Werk in der Handſchrifft durchzuſehen, und glauben, daß die Mühe des Herrn Verfaſſers nicht vergebens ſeyn werde, da es zumahl den Wunſch erfüllen hilft, daß wir von jedem heut zu Tage üblichen muſikaliſchen Inſtrumente ein bequemes und vollſtändiges Lehrbuch haben möchten. Es iſt zwar nicht jedermanns Ding, die Trompete zu blaſen, oder ſich mit Pauckenſchlagen abzugeben; aber einige Kenntniß von dieſen Künſten zu haben, kann leicht jedem Liebhaber der Muſik angenehm, und jedem Muſicus von Profeſſion, beſonders Componiſten nützlich ſeyn. Man findet außerdem in beſagtem Werke viel gute hiſtoriſche Umſtände geſammelt; wir wollen das Verzeichniß der Capitel hier einrücken, damit ein jeder von dem Inhalte des Werks ſelbſt urtheilen könne.

Cap. I. Von Erfindung und Beſchaffenheit der erſten Trompeten.

II. Von den vielfältigen Arten und Nahmen derſelben.

Cap. III.

Cap. III. Von dem alten Gebrauche der Trompeten, (als bey den Ebräern, Griechen und Römern.)

IV. Von dem neuen Gebrauche und Nutzen derſelben.

V. Von dem Misbrauche derſelben.

VI. Vom Anfatze, Einſtimmung und Veränderung der Trompeten, ſammt den darzu gehörigen Werkzeugen, als Mundſtück, Setzſtücken, Krumbogen und Sordun.

VII. Von den natürlichen Trompeten-Klängen, Intervallen und Verhältniſſen.

VIII. Von den heroiſchen Feldſtücken, Principal- und Taſelblaſen, ſammt der ſogenannten Zunge und Haue.

IX. Vom Klarin blaſen, was nehmlich gezogen, geſchleift, und geſtoſſen werden ſoll.

X. Von Bezeichnung und Ausdrucke der Trompeten-Manieren.

XI. Von Einrichtung der ſolennen Trompeter-Stücke.

XII. Von der ſehr-Art im Trompeten blaſen.

XIII. Von den prächtigen Paucken.

Anhang: Geſpräch zwiſchen dem Lehrherrn und Scholaren, von den Privilegien und Rechte der Trompeter, wie auch ſonſt nöthig zu wiſſenden Dingen und Materien.

Es wird auf dieſes Werk 16 gr. Pränumeration, ohne weitern Nachſchuß, angenommen; wenn es fertig iſt, wird es unter 1 Rthl. nicht verkauft werden. Wer 5 Exemplare zuſammen nimmt, erhält ſie für 1 holländiſchen vollwichtigen Ducaten. Man hat uns die Zeit, wenn der Druck vollendet ſeyn ſoll, und wie lange die Pränumeration angenommen wird, nicht gemeldet; man darf ſich aber dieſerwegen, ſo wie wegen der Pränumeration ſelbſt, nur an den Hrn Johann Ernſt Altenburg, Organiſten in Bitterfeld wenden.

Eee 3   Die

Facsimile of Hiller's announcement of Altenburg's essay. The upper portion of page 398 has been superimposed from page 397 to conserve space. The lower portion of page 398 and 399 are in their correct position. The page size has been reduced.

Trumpeters' and Kettledrummers' Art

Versuch einer Anleitung

zur

heroisch-musikalischen

Trompeter- und Pauker-Kunst,

zu mehrerer Aufnahme derselben

historisch, theoretisch und praktisch beschrieben

und mit Exempeln erläutert

von

Johann Ernst Altenburg.

Zwey Theile.

Halle,
gedruckt und verlegt bey Joh. Christ. Hendel.
1795.

Title page of the original edition, Halle 1795.

Essay on an Introduction

to the

Heroic and Musical

Trumpeters' and Kettledrummers' Art,

for the Sake of a Wider Acceptance of the Same,

Described Historically, Theoretically, and Practically

and Illustrated with Examples

by

Johann Ernst Altenburg

In Two Parts

Halle
Printed and Published by Joh. Christ. Hendel
1795

Complete English Translation
by

Edward H. Tarr

The Brass Press • *1974*

First published 1795
Copyright ©1974 by The Brass Press
First complete English translation published 1974

Library of Congress Cataloging in Publication Data

Altenburg, Johann Ernst, 1734-1801.
  Essay on an introduction to the heroic and musical trumpeters' and kettledrummers' art.

  Half title: Trumpeters' and kettledrummers' art.
  Translation of Versuch einer Anleitung zur heroischmusikalischen Trompeter–und Pauker–Kunst.
  1. Trumpet–Instruction and study–To 1800.
2. Kettledrum–Instruction and study–To 1800.
I. Title. II. Title: Trumpeters' and kettledrummers' art.

MT440.A613   788 .1'07   74-4026
ISBN O-914282-01-8

The Brass Press
159 Eighth Avenue North
Nashville, Tennessee 37203

Translator's Introduction

There are many sources from which information can be gained on matters pertaining to the Baroque trumpet, but none is as comprehensive as Johann Ernst Altenburg's treatise on the "heroic trumpeters' and kettle-drummers' art." [1] There are at least six areas in which thorough knowledge of his treatise is valuable for students of Baroque trumpet playing, be they musicologists or trumpeters.

In the first place, Altenburg discusses at length the use of the trumpet in former times, especially among the Hebrews. His central thesis—that trumpeters formerly enjoyed a socially exalted position—is employed to justify the elevated position of the trumpeter in the Baroque musical hierarchy. His insistence on the rightness of the trumpeters' high social standing runs through the entire treatise. Since Altenburg was writing during a period of great social upheaval, when courts were being dissolved one after the other and trumpeters were consequently becoming deprived of their basis of existence, his work is to be understood as a last defense of a passing social order. We also witness the decline of clarino playing at first hand, learning that the primary reason for this decline was change: change in the social order, and change in musical taste.

Second, one gains from the treatise considerable insight into the tightly-knit organization of the trumpeters of the Holy Roman Empire into guilds or

---

1 Altenburg was born on June 15, 1734 in Weissenfels and died on May 14, 1801 in Bitterfeld. The original German title of his treatise reads: *Versuch einer Anleitung zur heroisch-musikalischen Trompeter- und Pauker-Kunst.* It was published in Halle in 1795. Altenburg had submitted it in vain to the publisher Breitkopf a number of years before.

fellowships. These were in many respects the forerunners of today's musicians' unions. (Even the term *Kunstverwandte*, which literally means "relatives of art" and which we have translated as "brethren-in-art," echoes today in the salutations of official musicians'-union correspondence: "Dear Sir and Brother.") The trumpeters' fellowship, legally based on the authority of the Emperor and built on the hierarchy of his subordinates, was quite unique, as far as musicians' organizations of that time are concerned, and possessed considerable power. In particular, the training of future trumpeters was regulated as sternly as in any other trade. To prevent the number of trumpeters and kettledrummers from increasing uncontrollably, it was decreed that only he who had served in at least one military campaign, thus earning the honored title of Field Trumpeter or Kettledrummer, was allowed to take on a student. Only one pupil at a time was instructed, unless one's own sons were also involved.

Third, the system of training itself is discussed in great detail. A solid technical foundation was regarded as the musical base for the deserved social esteem. We learn that the relationship of teacher to pupil was much closer than it is today, and involved much more time. The pupil was actually an apprentice, lived with his master, and received instruction several times daily. In a series of nine lessons, Altenburg furthermore shows us how he would expect the two-year period of apprenticeship to progress; he proves himself thereby to be a highly skilled pedagogue.

Fourth, Altenburg makes some mention of musical instruments then and formerly in use, although we could wish for more completeness. On page 8, his assignment of Praetorius' *Jäger-Trommet* [2] to the ancient Romans is certainly a glaring error. It is curious that he did not associate the "so-called invention or Italian trumpet" (p. 11) with the shape of this very *Jägertrompete*. One recurrently finds references in other Baroque sources to Italian trumpets, which are said to have been coiled more often than German ones. Christoph Weigel, for example, discusses "a type of **coiled** trumpet" to which "the **Italian** or southern (*Welsche*) belong, which are wound around in a circle six times (*sechs mahlen rund herum gewunden*)." [3] We must conclude that the Italian or coiled trumpet—whether or not it had anything in common with Praetorius' *Jägertrompete*—was no longer in use in Altenburg's time, and that his observations were therefore not based on personal experience. On the other hand, Altenburg is admirably explicit in his description of the characteristics which a good trumpet must possess to be used in principale and clarino playing. Heavy silver trumpets, for instance, did not sound good at all, although they were often used for ceremonial purposes. A thick-walled instrument made of brass was termed suitable for principale playing, a thin-walled one suitable for clarino playing. Therefore, for general use, a compromise was recommended; the

2 *Syntagma Musicum* II (Wolfenbüttel 1619), Plate VIII, No. 11.
3 *Abbildung der gemein nützlichen Hauptstände* (Regensburg 1698), p. 232.

trumpets of the Haas family in Nuremberg were "generally considered to be the best" (p. 10). It was precisely this pronouncement of Altenburg's, among other reasons, which in 1968 moved the translator to choose trumpets made by a member of the Haas family as models for his reconstruction of Baroque trumpets.[4]

Fifth, Altenburg emphasizes the trumpeters' association with the military, transmitting to us valuable information on the structure and use of contemporary military signals. We can thus amplify our knowledge about the "field pieces" themselves, which are given in notation in earlier sources such as Thomsen (1598), Bendinelli (1614), and Mersenne (1636-37).[5]

In the sixth place, Altenburg is particularly valuable to us on matters of the correct style of execution. His discussion has two aspects: the affective and the technical. We would do well to read and re-read his remarks on pages 24-25 "On the Particular Use and Effect of the Trumpet." The basic affective content of trumpet tone is described as heroic. The trumpet makes the cavalry daring and bold; it can even incite to rage and fury, although the type of rage induced by the trumpet is carefully defined as less extreme than that "harmful rage" which man himself produces. Because of the major triad intrinsically possessed by the natural trumpet, this instrument can also induce joy and pleasure. However, "terrible and frightful is the sound of the trumpet . . . , for example: when it announces the approach of the enemy, when the enemy orders the handing over of a besieged city through a trumpeter, or when he captures it by storm to the din of the war trumpet" (p. 24). These rather specific associations would have been familiar to Baroque composers, and indeed we find the trumpet introduced in Baroque music only when one or the other of the above "affections" (*Affekte*) was to be expressed. It is interesting to note that Altenburg quotes the Roman author Horace part of the time, thereby looking to classical antiquity for his guide.

Altenburg discusses technical matters pertaining to style in great detail

---

4 These reconstructions of trumpets of Wolf Wilhelm Haas (1681-1760) are made by the West German firm, Meinl & Lauber. Joseph Wheeler—in the *Galpin Society Journal* XVIII (1965), p. 20—took exception to Altenburg's statement. He found English trumpets to be superior in workmanship to those of the Haas family or of other instrument-makers located in Nuremberg. However that may be, the fact remains that the most difficult trumpet parts ever written—by German or Austrian composers and, especially, composers active in Vienna between approximately 1730 and 1770—were not performed on English trumpets, but rather on trumpets made in Nuremberg or on others of a similar type. Besides, Altenburg is not talking about workmanship.

5 Magnus Thomsen, *Trompeterbuch,* in: *Trompeterfanfaren, Sonaten und Feldstücke,* edited by Georg Schünemann (Kassel 1936) (*Das Erbe deutscher Musik.* Erste Reihe, Reichsdenkmale, Band 7, Volume 1 of the section *Einstimmige Musik*). Cesare Bendinelli, *Tutta l'arte della Trombetta,* facsimile edition with closing remarks by Edward H. Tarr (Kassel, Basel, etc. 1974) (*Documenta musicologica*). Marin Mersenne, *Harmonie universelle,* facsimile edition with an introduction by François Lesure (Paris 1965).

in the last part of Chapter 10, in Chapter 11, and in Chapter 13. He repeats the well-known axiom that instrumentalists should try to imitate the human voice. His treatment of tonguing and huffing shows that both were subject to considerable nuance. His examples of huffing can be applied to the trumpet parts of J. S. Bach. Unequal articulation, explained by Dalla Casa in 1584 for the cornett and by Fantini in 1638 for the trumpet,[6] still applied to the trumpet in 1795. The interpretation of appoggiaturas and other compositional ornaments is also carefully explained. The performer is exhorted to add his own ornaments, tastefully and judiciously.

Altenburg prepared his work from various sources, the authors of which are mentioned in his preface. He may have become acquainted with many of these works through the generosity of the well-known musician, pedagogue, and theorist, Daniel Gottlob Türk (1750-1813), who allowed Altenburg to use his extensive library. One of Altenburg's most important sources, however, is not mentioned at all: the article "Trompeter" in Johann Heinrich Zedler's monumental, 64-volume *Grosses vollständiges Universal-Lexicon Aller Wissenschafften und Künste*.[7] It is surprising to find many of Altenburg's arguments already presented by Zedler, especially as regards the first part of the treatise. The similarity extends in some instances even to the duplication of quotations. (As Don Smithers has pointed out,[8] Zedler is also an important source for the oft-quoted Imperial Privileges of the trumpeters and kettledrummers of the Holy Roman Empire. They are published in full in Zedler, Vol. 45, col. 1122-1131.)

Zedler's article is one of the most important single sources, prior to Altenburg, concerning the trumpet. In addition, the entire lexicon was invaluable for the translator in deciphering cryptic terms such as the word *Verwandte* (in *Kunstverwandte*), used specifically to denote a fraternal relationship such as that found in guilds; *Dicasterium,* a high court; *Rostral* (from the Latin word *rastrum*), a type of many-tipped pen used to draw all five lines of the musical staff onto paper simultaneously; *Secret,* the privy seal of a potentate; and many others.

The need for an English translation of Altenburg's treatise has been apparent for some time. The widespread revival of interest in Baroque music and its proper execution has brought with it, more recently, a keen desire to know more about the Baroque trumpet. Within the past seven years there have been no less than five facsimile reprints of the original German edi-

6 Girolamo Dalla Casa, *Il vero modo di diminuir con tutte le sorti di stromenti* (Venice 1584), facsimile edition with a preface by Giuseppe Vecchi (Bologna 1970) (*Bibliotheca Musica Bononiensis,* Section II, No. 23). Girolamo Fantini, *Modo per imparare a sonare di tromba* (Frankfort 1638), facsimile edition by The Brass Press (Nashville 1972).

7 This lexicon appeared from 1732 through 1750, with four supplementary volumes in 1750-52. The article in question is on columns 1106-1131 of Vol. 45, which appeared in 1745.

8 "The Hapsburg Imperial *Trompeter* and *Heerpaucker* Privileges of 1653," *Galpin Society Journal* XXIV (1971), pp. 84-95.

tion of Altenburg's work.[9] Even for native speakers of German, however, the treatise presents problems of understanding. The sentences are often confusingly long; the style is pompous; and there are frequent grammatical errors and non sequiturs. How much more difficult, then, must the original treatise be for English-speaking readers!

The enterprising owner of The Brass Press, Stephen L. Glover, is therefore to be commended for recognizing the need for a translation and for encouraging such a task to be undertaken. I could not have carried it out, however, without the help of my wife—whose native language is German, and who did the preliminary translation of the entire Part One—and of my mother, a former English teacher of the old school, who is responsible for any elegance the finished product may possess. Mary Rasmussen's translation of most of Part Two, which appeared in 1958 in Volumes I and II of her admirable publication, Brass Quarterly, was also consulted; and although it is fairly free in places and occasionally inaccurate, it nevertheless served as a valuable foil in the preparation of the present translation.

Because of the many inconsistencies present in Altenburg's original text, a number of decisions had to be made by the translator as to the extent to which additions should be made to enhance intelligibility for the English reader. Such added words or phrases, whether they occur in the main text or the footnotes, were enclosed in square brackets, to distinguish them from Altenburg's own writing. At the same time, the overly long sentences of the Baroque German were often broken up into smaller ones. Although the attempt was made to translate as literally as possible so as to preserve the original flavor, it was not always feasible to retain some smaller words of little consequence such as "for" or "however"—words which may be characteristic for German but only detract from the sentence flow in English. (Altenburg loved to begin simple sentences with the conjunction *denn,* meaning "for," "because," or "since"—a conjunction which can be used in English only to begin a subordinate clause of a complex sentence. To have included every *denn* as Altenburg used it would have meant constructing dozens of still longer sentences, or leaving many sentences incomplete.) Since, however, the language of the Imperial Privileges was still more ceremonious than Altenburg's own, the long sentences of these documents were preserved wherever possible, with the aim of bringing out the contrast in style.

Numbers found in the margins of the present translation refer to the page numbers of the original German text. In the text of the translation, the names of notes lying in an indiscriminate octave are designated with capital letters in normal type, such as A, B, C, etc. Notes lying in specific octaves are written in italics, using the modern octave designation according

9 Bilthoven 1966, Kassel 1966, New York 1966, Amsterdam 1968, Leipzig 1972. The translator is in possession of the now-rare 1911 facsimile edition, which appeared in Dresden.

to which middle C is c'. The difference between this system and Altenburg's own is explained in footnote *a* to his page 68. German expressions in italic parentheses are editorial and serve as a guide to the translation. Altenburg's original footnotes were indicated with letters, which have been retained in this translation. The translator's footnotes have been numbered. The index has been prepared by Bruce R. Smedley.

Edward H. Tarr
Basel, Switzerland
Summer 1973

Dedicated to

the Most Serene Elector
and Duke,

Friedrich August,

Duke of Saxony, Juliers, Cleve, and Berg,
also of Engern and Westphalia,
Archmarshal and Elector of the Holy Roman Empire,
Landgrave of Thuringia,
Margrave of Meissen, also of Upper and Lower Lusatia,
Burgrave of Magdeburg,
Princely Count of Henneberg,
Count of the Mark, of Ravensberg, Barby, and Hanau,
Lord of Ravenstein, &c., &c.,

My most gracious Elector and Lord

Most Serene Elector and Duke,
Most Gracious Elector and Lord!

I believe that I dare to dedicate this treatise on the trumpeters' and kettle-drummers' art in humble submission to your forever **Electoral Highness** especially since **your Highness** not only protects the Arts and Sciences in general with great distinction, but also, as **Archmarshal** of the Holy Roman Empire, grants **his** exalted protection to the **field trumpeters** and **military kettledrummers** in particular. With this assumption I am hoping all the more [vi] surely for the gracious forbearance of **your Electoral Highness,** with the added wish that **your Highness** might recognize this Essay with benevolent reception.
    With most humble deference

Your Forever Electoral Highness'

most humble and obedient servant,
Johann Ernst Altenburg

Preface

Neither pride nor an author's vanity had any part in the making of this textbook; my only intention with it was, rather, to write a book in which the trumpeters' and kettledrummers' art would be taught more extensively than has been done so far in any publicly known instruction. Such instruction seemed to me all the more necessary since only very few practising musicians themselves understand the whole scope of the art under consideration. This may be mostly the reason why presently it is scarcely honored and recompensed by anyone any more. I will pass over other causes of its gradual decay in silence. The true artist knows these causes anyway; however, he for whom the appreciation *(Gefühl)* of music is something totally unknown is not in the habit of reading books about music. I may not hope, through this essay, to elevate the [trumpeters'] art once again, or herewith to have treated exhaustively everything pertaining to good trumpet playing; but I still flatter myself that I may perhaps draw the attention of a man of discernment to this branch of music which hitherto has been so badly neglected and encourage him herewith to take upon himself such a task.

Up until now, that which one finds here and there in writings about trumpets and kettledrums refers partly to their history, partly to their theory and use. However, all are only fragments, which strictly speaking do not form a whole, neither in this nor in that part of this science. It is a well-known fact that **Alardus, Athenaeus, Bartholini, Bulengerus, Baierus, Eustatius, Festus, Fesselius, Heineccius, Josephus, Knauth, Lipsius, Lundius, Ludovicus, Mersenne, Meibomius, Praetorius, Printz, Polyd., Virgilius, Reimmann, Sil. Italicus, Sprenger, Stewechius, Vegetius, Sal. van Til,** and others have written long ago about the invention, the changes, and the old use of trumpets and kettledrums, as well as of the advantages which brethren in this art *(Kunstverwandte)* formerly received. However, all this belongs to musical history. With newer writers, however—for instance in the works of **Büsing, Faber, Forkel, Galland, Mattheson, Mizler, Sorge, Schmidt,** and **Werkmeister**—one already finds something more, for some have examined the nature of the trumpet even mathematically. Among these, **Sorge** has especially distinguished himself.

A fine dissertation on the **rights** of trumpeters was written and expounded by Professor **Wildvogel** of Jena in the year 1711. The famous **Examining Society** *(prüfende Gesellschaft)* **of Halle**, as well, delivered two excellent treatises on this subject in 1741 and 1743. Moreover, in 1770 an anonymous [writer], presumably a privileged military kettledrummer, published in Leipzig, at his own expense, a small treatise with the following title: "Answer to the treatise on the use and misuse of kettledrums, printed in the *Musikalisch-Wöchentliche Nachrichten und Anmerkungen* in the year 1768, pp. 208-220." In this [answer] he attempts to refute [the ideas propounded by] the author of that article. I shall touch upon the most important [aspects] of all of these treatises at the proper place, for they all deserve more or less praise.

What I have accomplished in this essay, and where I may have failed, I wish [to learn] from the judgment of impartial scholars. I wish only that they, in judging this compendium, will consider that I am the first and only one up until now to seek to present and discuss not merely individual parts, as [did] my predecessors, but everything pertaining to the trumpeters' art. With regard to this [completeness], I believe not without reason that I may count upon some indulgence.

The works which I have consulted are mentioned in [this] treatise itself at the proper places. Furthermore, I am greatly indebted in many respects to Mr. **Türk**, musical director in Halle. With great generosity he entrusted me [with] various works from his extensive library for my own use.

In conclusion, I hope that this effort of mine may be somewhat useful, not only to those superiors who have trumpeters under their command, but also to the brethren-in-art themselves.

Bitterfeld, the 7th [day] of May, 1794

Contents

FIRST PART

Historical and Theoretical Instruction
for
Learning to Play Trumpets and Kettledrums

SECOND PART

Practical Instruction
for
Learning to Play Trumpets and Kettledrums,
Illustrated with Rules and Examples

Table of Illustrations

1 The mounted trumpeters and mounted kettledrummer are illustrations by Matthaeus
Merian from the book *Representation of the Princely Procession and Jousting Bout
Held in Stuttgart by His Serene Highness Johann Friedrich, Duke of Württemberg,
from March 10 to 17, 1616, on the Occasion of the Baptism of His Son.*
2 The illustration of Johann Caspar Altenburg's mouthpiece is the only illustration to
appear in the original 1795 edition of *Trumpeters' and Kettledrummers' Art.* The bore
outline has been retouched to enhance its appearance in this edition.
3 This illustration of the mounted Imperial trumpeters and kettledrummers is taken
from "The Triumph of Maximilian I" (completed in 1526) by Hans Burgkmair. This
wood-cut has been assigned, by both Meder and Benesch, to Leonard Beck.

Historical and Theoretical Instruction

for

Learning to Play Trumpets and Kettledrums

FIRST PART

"The Defeat of the Saracens" —detail of an engraving from 1737 by Jean Moyreau (1690-1762) after an original painting by Philips Wouwerman (1619-1668)

2

On the Origin, Invention, and Nature

of the First Trumpets,

as Well as the Various

Kinds, Names, and Forms Thereof

The German word **Trompete** is derived in several ways. Some trace it from the Greek word **tromos**, others from the Latin **tremor**, i.e., a trembling or vibrating—both namely because of its trembling or vibrating sound.[a] Others [derive it] from the French word **trompe**, i.e., an elephant's trunk, for since the long tubes and trumpets blown by the Romans had approximately the form of such a trunk at the end of the instrument, thus they formed from it the diminutive *trompette*, i.e., a small trunk.[b] Most, however, look for the origin in the Old German word **Tromm**, with which a sound, vibration, or noise made by the closing of the teeth is expressed; and thus the old word *Trommet* is said to have originated. Afterwards, merely for euphony's sake, the *p* is said to have been inserted, and in such a manner [the instrument] came to be called [a] *Trompete.*[c]

Now, as far as the **invention** of the trumpet is concerned, various opinions 2 thereon are expressed; some credit Jubal with it, others the Egyptians, and still others the Etruscans.

Lipsius mentions the use of the trumpet by the Egyptians and Achaeans. This [mention] simultaneously illuminates [the fact] that the [Egyptians] believed their idol Osiris [d] to be its inventor and that it was blown only by

a   Concerning this, see Jablonsky, *Allgemeines Lexicon der Künste und Wissenschaften,* as well as Fasch, *Kriegs-[,] Ingenieur- und Artillerie-Lexicon.* No less [important is] Hübner's *Natur-[,] Kunst- und Handlungs-Lexicon.*
b   See the engraving in Lipsius, *de mil[itia] Rom.,* Book IV, Dialogue X, as far as the [above-]mentioned similarity is concerned.
c   [Der] Spate [pseudonym for Kaspar Stieler, 1632-1707] in [*Der Teutschen Stammbaum und Fortwachs, oder Teutscher*] *Sprachschatz* [. . . (Nürnberg 1691), in the chapter] on the origin of words.
d   He is said to have been the first Egyptian king, whom they worshipped like a god.

priests at sacrifices,[e] while the [Achaeans], on the other hand—one of the oldest Greek nations—attributed this invention to Minerva.

Among the Etruscans, sometimes Piseus, sometimes Maleus, often Tyrsenus, as well as Tyrzaeus or Tyrtaeus, is named as the inventor thereof.

According to **Pliny**,[f] **Piseus**, an Etruscan king, is supposed to be the inventor of the trumpet in the year 2951 of the creation of the world, or 260 years before the founding of Rome; and according to Alexander Sardus, [it was] **Maleus** or **Mileus**, an Etruscan general. **Virgil**, too, says,[g] "and the Tyrrhenian turmoil of the trumpet roared through the air." **Pausanias** credits **Tyrsenus**, son of Hercules [and] a general of the Etruscans, with [the invention]. **Diodorus Siculus**[h] writes the following about it: "The Etruscans, who were strong in infantry, introduced the first trumpet because it was very useful to them in war." **Acron**, in writing about Horace's poetic art, wishes to prove that the poet Tyrtaeus, who lived in the year of the world 3314, must have produced it, and **Porphirius** wishes to credit him at least with the creation of a certain melody [and of a certain] manner of playing it. Also **Justinius**[i] agrees with the latter and tells of the occasion on which [Tyrtaeus] is said to have first used it and made himself famous with it:

3
> As, namely, the Spartans,[1] at war with the Messenians, called on their god Apollo for advice, they received the answer from him that if they wanted to hold the field, they should avail themselves of [the services of] an Athenian general. Now since the Athenians were thus supplicated by the Spartans, they sent them this very Tyrzaeus,[k] who was a lame, one-eyed, ugly man, just in order to mock them. The Spartans, however, made use of his help despite this [mockery], and made him their general, since they well knew that an intelligent and heroic spirit might sometimes be hidden [even] in a misshapen body. This [Tyrzaeus] immediately instructed many of them in trumpet-playing and stood at the head of the army himself. Now when the battle was beginning, he ordered [an] alarm to be blown everywhere, and through such an unprecedented and unusual sound the Messenians became frightened and fled in panic; whereby the Spartans thus easily gained a great victory over them.[l]

e   The period from the Flood until the exodus of the Israelites from Egypt is reckoned by historians to be 796 years. See Hübner's *Geographische Historie*.
f   In his *Hist. natur.*, Book VII, Chapter 56.
g   *Aeneid*, Book VIII.
h   In his *Histor. Biblioth.*, Book VI.
i   Book III, p. 53.
1   Altenburg writes "Lacedaemonians."
k   Printz in his *Musik. Hist.* calls this Tyrzaeus a famous trumpeter and elegy writer. Hübner in his *Politische Historie*, p. 197, lists him even as a king of the Messenians —which is probably an error, however—saying at the same time that he had formerly been a lame, one-eyed schoolmaster, who animated the soldiers to battle by his heroic poems.
l   Athens, Messenia, and Sparta [translator's note: Altenburg writes "Lacedaemon"] were nothing but little Greek kingdoms until all Greece and Persia became [united into] a monarchy in the year [of the world] 3619 by Alexander the Great.

All these divergent opinions arise from nothing else than the various changes to which the trumpet has been exposed, as I will presently show; [they come] as well from other similar wind instruments, as well as in the manner of playing them. The inventions of many things can be found in the writings of ancient scribes—especially in Polydor [and] Virgil—[inventions] which are rather to be considered as changes or improvements, especially so since all the world's arts and sciences have grown from only very small beginnings.

The heathen had the custom of crediting their gods with the invention of their arts, and thence they attributed music to Apollo. [The writers] Vossius, Hegezius, and Heydeger also show beyond a doubt that [the heathen] made Apollo out of Jubal.

That the trumpet is among the very oldest inventions can be deduced from [the fact] that it was already known in the time of Moses, who was born in the year of the world 2372. Moses had two silver trumpets made and [he] presented them to the priests **Eleazar** and **Ithamar**, sons of **Aaron**, with the intention that they should introduce them in a solemn ceremony at a religious service to be held outdoors. At the same time he taught the Israelites that the trumpet was an instrument hallowed by God, and that for precisely that reason, only the priests were to be allowed to play it. He did so in order to make that superstitious people—whose grasp of religion could be preserved only by direct impression on the senses— more ardent, respectful, steadfast, and devoted in their religion. Thus the [idea] developed that a layman could play any instrument except the trumpet, because [playing that instrument except by the priesthood] would be a desecration of divinity.

In the Hebrew Scriptures is found the word **chazozrah**, which **Luther** translates as *Trommete*,[m] as opposed to **jobel** [and] **keren** (Chaldean **shofar**), which are [rendered] by scholars as cornetts, trombones, [and] ram's horns, of which Jubal is named as the inventor.[n,o]

Josephus,[p] the first historian, and several others, describe [the **chazozrah**] as an instrument one ell long, chased from heavy metal, [an instrument] which expands gradually from the mouthpiece to the end in the form of a bell *(Glocke)*.

In the desert, the trumpets were presumably kept in the hut of Moses, or in [those of] the sons of Aaron. According to **Josephus** and **Lundius**,

m Except for I Chronicles 13:8, where he probably erred in translating it as *Posaune*.
n Genesis 4:21.
o Precisely this instrument-inventor Jubal is said to have received his name from the instrument, the jobel. He is also considered to be the inventor *(Angeber)* of zithers and psaltery *(Zittern und Psalter)*. [Translator's note: Luther says (Genesis 4:21): *"von dem sind hergekommen die Geiger und Pfeifer,"* and the King James Bible calls him "the father of all such as handle the harp and organ."]
p *de Antiq. Iudaeo,* Book III, Chapter 1.

there were fifteen steps on each side of the vestibule of the temple, where all the musical instruments were hung up, the trumpets included.

5   Thus then, real trumpets differ from trombones and ram's horns, according to name, use, and tone as well as in form and material. Trumpets were peculiar only to priests and were designated for a sacred and solemn use, whereas trombones and ram's horns were allowed to be played by ordinary people. The tone of the former was pure and clear but that of the latter coarse and dull. The former went out straight, the latter were bent in a curve. The former were of silver, the latter from a ram's horn or [of a] lesser metal.

Furthermore, we know that these trumpets doubtlessly underwent more changes than any other musical instruments of warfare. Although they were introduced after a time to other known peoples, most of these gave them a different shape. It is probably for this reason that many claim to be the inventor. The foreign and Oriental peoples especially have given [the trumpet] quite peculiar shapes, as one may see particularly in **Agricola** and **Praetorius**.

Eustatius mentions six kinds of wind instruments in heathen history which were then in use: (1) The **cnophe**, invented by **Osiris** and played by the Egyptians, [was] used at sacrifices. (2) The **salpinxathina**, invented by **Minerva**, [was] used by the Achaeans. (3) The **cernix** [was] used by the Gauls. (At the top it had a leaden tube which served as a mouthpiece; at the bottom [where the air] leaves [the instrument] it had the shape of an animal. It had, incidentally, a sharp tone.) (4) The **Paphlagonian** [trumpets resembled] the head of an ox at the bottom and had a sound similar to the lowing of the ox itself. (5) The **Median** [trumpets were] made out of reed [and had] a low tone. (6) The **Etruscan** [trumpets were] similar to a Phrygian pipe, with a split *(gespalten)* mouthpiece and a sharp sound; these were in fashion with the Romans, as **Eustatius** maintains, referring in this matter to Diod. Sicul.

Further differentiation of these wind instruments, moreover, is made not only in their shape and [number of] coils, but also in the material of which they are made.

6   Trumpets made of silver, brass, tin, copper, porcelain, glass, clay, wood and such, all have a trumpet-like sound inasmuch as they all produce the trumpet intervals correctly, except that one [trumpet] may sound purer and clearer, stronger or weaker, higher or lower, duller and coarser than another. Therefore, an [instrument-]maker must be particular not only about the selection of a good, pure metal, but also about the proper joining thereof. Much depends on these [two factors], with respect to the purity and clarity [of the] sound as well as to the ease of playing [the instrument], since the air particles are herewith more easily moved back and forth vibrated, and in this way made to sound.

Even though our present-day wind instruments are already well enough known in themselves to make a long discussion superfluous, there will be nevertheless many [people] who do not pay precise attention to the various types thereof. Otherwise [these wind instruments] would certainly be better classified and distinguished in higher and lower categories, as they were by musicians of old. We have so many kinds and types thereof that we could well do without some of them; some [instruments] are used in one [place], others in another.

I shall endeavor to distinguish the kinds of trumpets one from another in a rational manner. I will thus divide them mainly into two principal categories, namely into **old** and **new**, and these again into various subordinate classes or types.

A. The Old Kind [of Trumpets]

First Class

(1) The **two silver trumpets** (*tuba antiqua ebraea*) made by Moses, which I have already mentioned above, are without doubt the noblest.
Painters and sculptors generally like to present and depict both Fame [q] and the Archangel Gabriel [r] with such trumpets.

(2) The **ram's horn** (Hebrew *jobel* or *keren*, Chald. *shofar*) was a wind   7 instrument made out of the horn of a ram or other animal [and] used by the ancient Hebrews on various occasions, even unimportant ones, as we know from Holy Scriptures. [s]

(3) Still another instrument [2] (Lat. *buccina*, so called from *bucca* and *cano*) was used by musicians of old. It was actually a musical instrument of war which they used particularly for giving the signal for attack, departure, and retreat. It was made out of ore [*sic*] or metal and was completely coiled, whereby it differed from the *tuba directa*, which was straight. [t]

There is very little information available about the form and structure of the trumpets of the Greeks, although we know that they used them frequently. However, I do not doubt that they would certainly have retained the three mentioned kinds—[a supposition] which is all the more likely because of the many wars they waged among themselves. Galland, too, informs us that the above-mentioned three wind instruments of the Hebrews were not handed down to the Romans, mentioning especially

q [She] was the goddess of fame with the heathen.
r [He] is set above the trumpeters as their patron saint.
s See Bartholocius, *Biblioth. Rab.*, Part 2, p. 186 ff., and Hedrich's *Lexic.*
2 Altenburg writes "Still another *trombone*," showing that he did not consider the *buccina* to be a true trumpet. (See the first paragraph on p. 5.)
t See Printz, *mus. Hist.*, Chapter 3, p. 30.

three kinds which were common with the ancient Romans, namely:

Second Class

(1) *Tuba* (otherwise *tuba directa*), from *tubus*, i.e., a tube, because with its straight form it resembled a tube.

(2) *Lituus*, [which] was a bit smaller, curved toward the end, and intended especially for the cavalry—just as, on the contrary, the former was intended more for the infantry.

(3) *Buccina*, which was curved all the way around and [was] common to everybody.

From the treatise by **Praetorius** [u] on the *Tuba Hieronymi* we gather that after some time there were several such wind instruments in use by the Romans as well as a horn,[v] [which was] wound tightly many times and is mentioned by him under the name *Jäger-Trommet*. [The Romans] also had one in the form of a dragon's head coiled around like a horn, named *tromba corva*. Still other such types [of the Romans] were the *tromba doppia*, [*tromba*] *spezzata*[,] *clareta*, etc.

With the Orientals, too, various wind instruments were introduced as follows:

Third Class

(1) **Kerena**, a trumpet of the East Indians, fifteen feet long.[w]

(2) **Kereney**, [a] trumpet in Ispahan, twelve ells long, [made] of copper, with such a big bell at the bottom that it almost resembles a big bowl, on which they rather roared than blew.[x]

(3) **Nafiri**, another type of trumpet customarily used in the East Indies.[y]

(4) **Tre**, [the name of] the Siamese trumpet, supposedly made out of wood, in a straight form and wound round with golden rings.[z]

(5) **Ja**, a similar trumpet of immense size which is said to be used by the Mongols and Tartars.

At the time before the trumpet became customary with the Teutons, they emboldened themselves at war, as we can read, with the sound of their

---

u In his *mus. Hist.*, Table VIII, Figure 10. [His *Syntagma musicum II*, of course, is meant.]

v *Ibid.*, Table 8, Figure 11.

w See Bonnet in his *Hist. de la Mus.*, Chapter III, p. 326.

x See *die neue Welthistorie*, Volume III, p. 347.

y See Walther, *mus. Lexicon*, p. 437.

z See de la Loubère, *Beschreib. des Königr. Siam.*

weapons only. At the attack this [sound] consisted partly in screaming terribly, and partly in beating on their hollow shields.[a] Later, according to the account of Vegetius, they introduced horns of buffalo and aurochs which were mounted with silver at the mouthpiece *(Ansatz)*. The Saxon emperor **Heinrich I**, with the surname **Auceps**, reigned from 919 to 936. He ordered tournaments and jousting-bouts. Subsequently, probably in the middle of the century, trumpets came into use with the Germans as particularly appropriate instruments to that end. [This circumstance] seems to be all the more confirmed through [the fact] that the descriptions of these jousting-bouts frequently mention the sounding *(Aufblasen)* of trumpets. Nevertheless, contrary to this opinion, some people claim that the Germans at that time learned and took over not only these games, but also the use of the trumpet from the French.

Be that as it may, this much is certain: [trumpets] became customary with us, little by little, only during the Middle Ages *(in den mittlern Zeiten),* as I will mention further below.

Our ordinary trumpet (Lat. *tuba,* French *trompette,* Ital. *tromba* or *clarino*) is known as a musical wind- and war-instrument and is used especially by the cavalry.

Its sound inspires courage; [it] is penetrating and sharp—as piercing, as it were, in the high register as it is blaring in the low. It is heard the farthest of all instruments and is thus named the Queen over all the others. **Mattheson** [b] calls it the far-sounding and heroic, **Schmidt** [c] the jubilating trumpet.

This [kind of] trumpet is, as a rule, made of chased silver or brass and composed of six parts which form three principal elongated tubes. Toward the end it becomes enlarged like a funnel, and a mouthpiece with a small opening proportioned to [the size of] the narrow tube is put onto it. Instrument makers know, for the most part, only *ex praxi* [how] to give them the correct length and diameter. However, [they] seldom [base these measurements] on true mathematical reasoning as [they] should. It is because of this very fact that trumpets made by different makers rarely sound perfectly in tune together, although other causes are also responsible for this [situation].

The silver trumpets used on ceremonial occasions at the large courts are commonly made out of so-called Augsburg silver.[3] However, the opinion

9

10

a   Tacitus, *d[e origine, situ,]* m[*oribus ac populis*] G[*ermanorum*], Chapter 3.
b   In [*Das neu-eröffnete*] *Orchestre,* p. 265. [Altenburg writes "Matheson."]
c   In *Theol. Musika* [sic].
3   Altenburg speaks of *"Augspurger 13 löthigem Silber."* Silver cannot be worked if it is pure. For this reason, copper was added to the silver to form an alloy. According to Zedler (see Preface), the purest alloys—those of Paris and Augsburg —contained 14 parts of silver and 2 parts of copper. In another place, he describes the Augsburg alloy as 13-*löthig,* the purity also mentioned by Altenburg. The part was called a *Loth.* Alloys of diminishing purity, down to 10 parts of silver and 6 of copper, were allowed.

that these are superior in sound to those of brass is unfounded. Rather the contrary is proven by experience. Presumably, the cause thereof lies with the compactness of the silver, which cannot be chased as well as brass.

With any trumpet the following three properties are mainly to be observed: (1) its length or shortness, (2) [the] width or narrowness [of its bore], and (3) the strength or weakness of the material. I shall touch upon the most important of these.

A **long** [trumpet] is **low**, and a **short** [trumpet] **high** in pitch. [According to the highness or lowness of pitch, a given trumpet has various registers;] these [registers] receive different names, which will be dealt with more closely later on.

A wide [bore] trumpet may sound more powerful and more penetrating than [one with] a narrow bore, just as a horn in E♭ or D♯ produces a weak, low, expressive sound on account of the narrowness and length of its body; however, [the wider bore] also demands a stronger thrust of air.

A trumpet of strong thick metal may be durable and useful for field-piece *(Feldstück)* and principale *(Principal)* playing; but in the high register towards the clarino *(Clarin)* it demands more wind, has an unpleasant sound, and therefore is altogether unsuitable for a clarino player *(Clarinist)* and concert trumpeter. However, if the metal is too thin and weak, it is true that [such a trumpet] can be played easily in the high register and has a [more] pleasant tone than [one of heavy metal]; but it is not strong and penetrating enough in the low register for field piece and principale playing, and not at all durable.

For common use, therefore, a medium kind of metal is the best. However, if another [person] should want to employ a stronger type for principale and a weaker type for clarino [playing], according to the nature of the part he has to play, he would not be incorrect. Be that as it may, those [trumpets] made by J. W. Haas [4] in Nuremberg and set with angel-heads are commonly held to be the best. The present observations, which any expert trumpeter can make for himself, are simply the results of our own experience.

11   I have already said that the difference[s] between our common trumpets consist only in the length and size, which brings us to [the new kind.]

B. The New Kind

First Class

(1) Without a doubt, the choir-pitched C trumpet has priority with us Germans. It is so called because it is or should be in the pitch of C

---

4 Altenburg writes "W. Hasen."

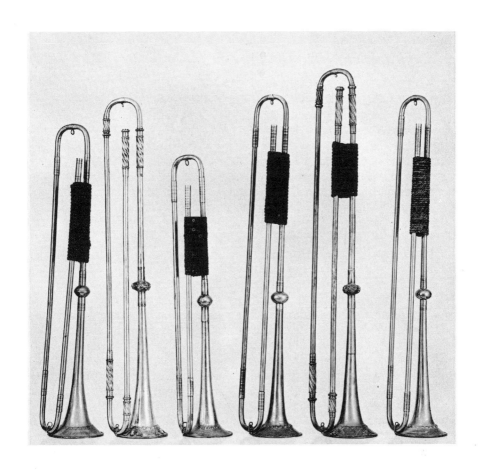

Six trumpets made by the Haas family, from the Bernoulli collection (Greifensee, Switzerland). From left to right, the first three were made by Johann Wilhelm Haas (1649-1723), the founder of the dynasty, the following two by Wolf Wilhelm Haas (1681-1760), and the remaining one by Ernst Johann Conrad Haas (1723-1792). Note that the second and fifth trumpets have angel-heads on the bell garland. They also possess heavy cast ferrules with a spiral pattern, and a cast ball with angel-heads. The remaining trumpets are of a lighter, simpler construction. (Photograph: Photo Hoffmann, Basel.)

11

with the organ (which commonly is in choir pitch). Therefore, according to the normal foot-tone *(Fusston)* it must be of equal length with the low pipe of the diapason; i.e., it must be exactly 4 ells or 8 feet long, if it is indeed to tune up correctly.[d] Since, as a rule, choir and chamber pitch differ from each other by only one tone, in that the former is a tone higher and the latter a tone lower,[5] it is easily understood that this [choir-pitched C] trumpet, according to chamber pitch, [will sound] in the key of D. Therefore it can just as easily be called the chamber-pitched D trumpet, although some are also pitched in E♭. With this type it is quite comfortable to play field pieces and the principale [part] in the low register as well as [the] clarino [part] in the high register, in that this [choir-pitched C trumpet] is not too long for the former and not too short for the latter. [Being able to play this kind of trumpet] is of no small advantage to the art of the German trumpeters.

(2) The chamber-pitched F or French trumpet, [so called] because it is used by the French, is somewhat shorter; therefore, [it is pitched] a minor third, or one and a half tones higher than the former.

(3) The chamber-pitched G or English trumpet (*tromba piccola* in Italian) is so called because it is customarily used by the English. It is a whole tone higher still than the former [or French trumpet] and a fourth (*Diatessaron*) higher than the first. Clarino playing cannot be pushed quite as high with it as on the German D trumpet, and the player tires faster [on account] of its short body. Field pieces and principale parts can be played very penetratingly and blaringly with it.

12   The further difference[s] of these wind instruments come not only from the variations in size, but also from the more frequent coiling, the form, and the material thereof.

Second Class

(1) Here the so-called invention *(Inventions-)* or Italian trumpet presumably merits first mention, since the construction *(inventirt)* [of this instrument], with its more frequent coils, [makes it] comfortable [to hold]. It is used mainly in Italy, has the same trumpet sound as the

---

d   This is true only for an eight-foot *Principal* in the organ *(und Orgelwerke)*. There are also similar trumpets which are a half tone higher. However, we are not discussing these here.

5   In Altenburg's time, choir pitch was higher than chamber pitch. In former times, and in some places, the relationship of the two pitches was sometimes reversed. See Altenburg's own discussion in the Second Part, Chapter 9, as well as the article "Kammerton" in the *Riemann Musiklexikon,* Sachteil (Mainz 1967), pp. 435-436.

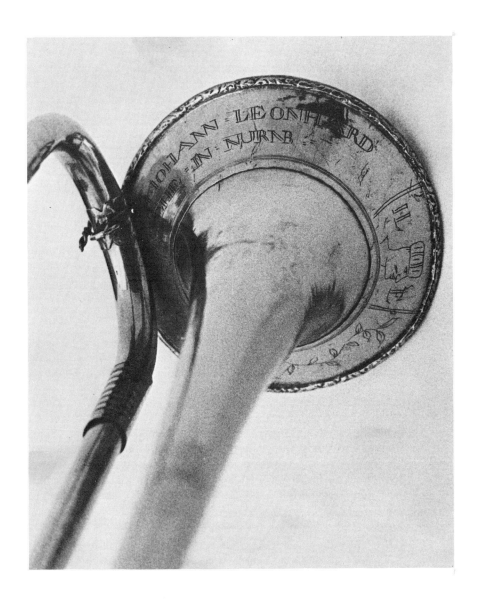

Bell of a trumpet by Johann Leonhard Ehe II (1663-1724), in the translator's collection. Inscription: M[ACHTS] IOHANN LEONHARD EHE IN NURN-B[ERG]. Pitch: slightly lower than modern D. (Photograph: Christopher Broder-sen, Sehmsdorf, West Germany.)

13

above-mentioned, and comes in various sizes.
It is not used by the cavalry trumpeters, but [rather] by the so
called oboists and regimental fifers of the infantry.

(2) The slide trumpet, which is commonly used by tower watchme
(Thürmer) and by city musicians *(Kunstpfeifer)* for playing chorale
(geistliche Lieder), is constructed almost like a small alto trombon
because it is pulled back and forth during playing, whereby [th
player] can easily bring forth the missing tones [of the harmoni
series].[6]

(3) The clarinet, which actually means little trumpet *(Trompetchen)*, wa
invented at the beginning of this century by a certain artist fror
Nuremberg. It is of various sizes.
This wooden wind instrument is not unlike an oboe and has a broa
mouthpiece attached in front. Its range extends as a rule from f t
d'', although some ascend as high as f''—consequently, thre
whole octaves. [It can] also be played chromatically, since it i
provided with all half tones, and can thus modulate to a multitud
of keys and play along in them. This may have motivated some com
posers to write special concertos and sonatas for [this instrument]. It
sharp and penetrating sound is of good service, particularly in th
military music of the infantry, and it sounds much better from afa
than from close up.

(4) The marine trumpet is not properly a wind [instrument]; it is rathe
an ancient sea instrument still used by sailors. In shape and desig
it is a long, hollowed-out [piece of] wood strung with a catgut string
[It is] usually played with a bow and renders the entire range o
trumpet tones. For this reason, it can also be used as a *monochord* t
measure [intervals of] sound.[e]

(5) The trumpet in the organ is a specific register belonging to the reeds
Attempts to put it into either the manual or the pedals have failed
Just as organ-builders are unable to reproduce naturally the sound o
the human voice, so will they also be unable to imitate [the sound of
the trumpet properly.[f]

6 This is the *tromba da tirarsi* or German slide trumpet, for which Bach, amon
others, composed. It is the descendant of the instrument seen in the hands c
angel musicians in the pictorial art of the fifteenth and sixteenth centuries
Attached to the mouthpiece, and inside the first yard (or length of tubing), is
mouthpipe upon which the entire instrument slides back and forth. A specimer
by Huns Veit of Naumburg, dated 1651, is preserved as no. 639 of the Berli
musical instrument collection. On the English slide trumpet of the seventeent
century and more particularly the nineteenth, the entire bend of tubing neares
the player was moved.

e Concerning this, see de Chales, *Mund. mathem.*, Part III, p. 23, and Gon
[Filippo] Bon[anni], *Gab[inetto] Arm[onico]*, where its divisions are to be seen.

f It [seems] most peculiar, [even] absurd, that these attempts [to imitate the soun
of the human voice and of the trumpet on the organ] are made on a reed stor
even though neither the voice nor the trumpet seems to be intrinsically reedy.

Finally, Mr. **Adelung** [g] reports in his *Musikal. Gelahrtheit* that in 1723 Mr. **Gleichmann**, then city organist in Jimenau, invented a certain kind of trumpet that [was so small it] could be [concealed] in leather gloves or put into one's pocket. Since, however, nothing further has been heard of it since that time, this invention will presumably have been of little importance.

g Professor, and simultaneously organist at the *Predigerkirche* in Erfurt.

Chapter 2

On the Ancient Usage of the Trumpet, and the Dignity and Advantages Which Trumpeters Have Always Enjoyed

According to history, the two silver trumpets given to the priests by Moses are the oldest known to us.

It is also certain that they were used principally for solemnity in the outside service.

14 In the Old Testament we find that trumpets were played to call the assembly together and at the decampment of the army.[h]

Fesselius comments upon this in his Biblical concordance with passages [from the] Old Testament and ascribes their use to the following two circumstances:

> I. **For the gathering of the entire assembly**, when **both** [were Blown]; or for the gathering of the princes and generals, when only **one** was Blown [i] *(schlecht geblasen)*.[7] The latter had their particular gatherings to which the people were not admitted; at the gathering[s] of the assembly, however, they always had to be present.
>
> II. **At the breaking of [the] camp[s]** (α) that lie on the east parts, when the priests Sounded an Alarm *(trommeteten)*[7] for the first time, and

h   In Numbers 10:2.
i   *Ibid.*, verses 3-4.
7   Luther translated the Hebrew expression *tĕḳiʿā* as *"schlecht blasen"* (i.e. *"schlicht blasen"*), which the King James Bible renders as "blow." The other expression, *tĕrûʿāh*, was rendered by Luther as *"drommeten"* and by the King James Bible as "blow an alarm" (Numbers 10:5-6) and "sound an alarm" (Numbers 10:7). I have capitalized the English expressions in the translation of Altenburg's text, in order to set them off as specific techniques of playing the trumpet associated with the Hebrews. For the most up-to-date information on Hebrew trumpet calls and their appearance in modern notation, see David Wulstan, "The Sounding of the Shofar", *Galpin Society Journal* XXVI (1973), pp. 29-46.

16

(β) [of those] that lie on the south side, when it happened for the second time.[k]

The differentiating signal was thus given partly through the number of trumpets, partly through the manner of playing them. The former differentiated between the gathering[s] of the entire assembly [and those of] the princes and generals; the latter, however, when camp was breaking, indicated the direction of the camp. At the breaking of camp, therefore, they always Sounded an Alarm, but at the gathering[s], they just Blew.

The so-called **Blowing** was a constant, unbroken sound, whereby a certain tone was sustained for a rather long time, and was a sign for peace of mind.[1] **Sounding an Alarm**, however—a broken and modulated sound caused by the interchanging of various tones and by blaring—indicated a joyful, warlike affection *(Affect)*.[m]

Hereby it should be mentioned in addition that the Blowing was done by one [trumpeter] alone or by two at the same time, whereas the Sounding of an Alarm was always carried out by two. This difference was quite necessary, so that everyone could immediately understand the meaning of the sound. Although, with the breaking of camp, the tabernacle would be dismantled at the first call, the priests were nevertheless able within a certain span of time to give four particular signals with the trumpets, so that every branch of the people could gather and take its [proper] place.

Directions were ordinarily given to these trumpeting priests by the high priest, **Eleazar**. In wartime, they were subordinated to the military priest, who was anointed and ordained to war.[n]

Their places and positions differed according to the occasion. Ordinarily, they stood near the tabernacle, where the priest performed his office. In camp, however, after there was no more tabernacle, they played in front of the army commander's tent. We never find them standing on the singing platform next to the other Levites who were appointed to sing and play. The trumpeting priests, [who] were almost always with the king, wore

15

---

k [Numbers 10:] 5 and 6.
l *Roschi Hasch.,* Chapter 8.
m Memon in *H. Schophar,* Chapter III, § 4. [We have translated the word *Affect* with "affection," that is, a "particular movement of the spirit and of the senses" (Zedler). The Baroque doctrine of affections was derived from Aristotle's teaching. According to Baroque thought, the affections were particular states of the body and/or of the mind induced by the distribution of fluids within the body. The principal affections were: love, joy, yearning, hope, rage, hate, boldness, fear, and sadness. The minor affections were: favor, confidence, mercy, thankfulness, modesty, envy, shame, emulation, and desperation. (See Zedler.) "Affection" and "passion" are virtually synonymous. In a narrower sense, "affection" refers to the state of the body, "passion" to the state of the mind. As can be seen, affections or passions were not the same as emotions. For a succinct discussion of this matter, see Claude Palisca, *Baroque Music* (Englewood Cliffs, New Jersey, 1968), pp. 3-4.]
n Numbers 31:6.

magnificent garb,[o] and were, at that time, completely separated from common horn players, who were only allowed to play on their trombones and ram's horns outside the Temple. Consequently, these [priests] were invested with the name of "holy trumpeters." When, in battle, the Hebrews were attacked by the enemy, [all] the priests stood at the very front, at the head of the battle formation.[p] At sacrifice, [they stood] at the table on two pillars, or else near the Ark of the Covenant.[q] On these questions, see M. Semler, in his treatise on the Antiquities, in question and answer.

The **motives** prompting them to play the trumpets were, for instance, the following: (1) to glorify God; (2) to show thereby that they were a holy people [r] and soldiers of the Lord;[s] (3) to encourage the soldiers and make them more ardent thereby; [t] (4) to unite prayer with sonority; [u] [and] (5) to remind the people of the presence and assistance of God [so that they might] begin a battle trusting in Him.[v] [In this last case] they were supposed to regard the trumpet sound only as an outward sign of the assurance of Divine aid.

In the beginning, the silver trumpets were used only near the tabernacle and in encampment. However, when the Israelites came into the land of Canaan forty years later, within which time the number of both priests and trumpets had increased, they were using them as well for celebrations and other entertainments.

King **Solomon**, as told by **Josephus**,[w] is said to have had twenty thousand [trumpets] made for use in the Temple in Jerusalem, and only the priests were allowed to play them. However, this number appears grossly exaggerated and suspicious to **Raschius** *ad Succa.*[x]

They were played at all other solemnities, such as: (1) At the fixed feast days and new moons, for which reason [such occasions] were also called "trumpet days." [y] (2) At sacrifices, ordinarily taking place eighteen times a

---

o   Exodus 28:29. [Altenburg writes: "28 and 29."]
p   II Chronicles 13:12. [In Luther's translation of the Bible, God, his priests, and the *"Halldrommeten"* are said to be at the head (*"an der Spitze"*) of the battle formation, whereas in the King James Bible, it is merely stated: "And, behold, God himself is with us for our captain, and his priests with sounding trumpets to cry alarm against you." No reference is made here, in the King James version, to the priests' being at the *head* of the battle formation.]
q   I Chronicles 16:6.
r   [Altenburg states in his footnote that this verse is from Deuteronomy 19:6. However, it is found in Exodus 19:6. Trumpets are not mentioned.]
s   I Samuel 18:17 and 25:28. [Here the trumpet is not mentioned, however.]
t   II Chronicles 13:12.
u   II Chronicles 13:14.
v   Numbers 10:9.
w   Book VIII, Chapter 2.
x   Chapter X, *m.* 4. [Altenburg writes *"Dachsius."*]
y   Numbers 29:1. [Although the "trumpet days" are only mentioned indirectly in the King James Bible ("it is a day of blowing the trumpets unto you"), Luther speaks specifically of *"euer Drommetentag."*]

day (nine times at the morning and nine times at the evening sacrifice)[z] as well as at the food, drink, and fire sacrifices—here the sound was first sustained, then broken, and finally sustained again, as in the Temple.[a] (3) At the establishment and renewal of the Covenant with God. (4) At public services in general, and particularly during the singing of the Psalms. These were usually divided into three parts, and the priests sounded the trumpets between them. (This [sounding of trumpets] took place especially at the 17 word **Selah**, which actually marked a change of melody, and no less [often] at the word **Amen**. This [word] was understood by the people [to mean] Divine assent and [an] assurance that their prayers [would be answered].[b] [The people] then fell to earth on their faces before God.) (5) At the coronation of kings. (6) At the leading away of the Ark of the Covenant from the house of Abi Nadab to Obed Edom, [when] **seven priests** at once played on trumpets. (7) At the dedication of Solomon's Temple, that king [having] had **one hundred twenty priests** play [trumpets] simultaneously.

The trombones and ram's horns were played on various but far less important occasions, such as: (1) At some small celebrations, especially at the new moon and for the New Year (the latter occurred on the first day of the month Tishri, which was the first month of the civil year), as well as for the announcement of jubilee and celebration years. (2) To indicate the Sabbath. As a rule, the school headmaster (*chazan*) used to play at the beginning and end of the Sabbath from an elevated place—whence our tower playing is said to have originated.[c] (3) At the distribution of alms, [when] the Pharisees usually had [the trombones] play in front of them with a broken sound so that the people should gather together.[d] (4) At an excommunication—when Jesus Hannozeri was expelled from the community, they had forty trombones play simultaneously;[e] also, when King Judah was angry at a man for having taken meat at the market from Judah's son Ezechiel and the head of the academy, [the King] had trombones play and he excommunicated [the thief].[f] (5) When someone was to be executed, the fact being made public through the sound of the trombone. (6) At the opening of the gates, which was done three times a day.[g] (7) At a siege, [when] they played [an] alarm *(Lerm)*. (8) When they were attacked and 18 assaulted by enemies, [when] the watchmen on the walls and at the guard-stations *(Wache)* played [an] alarm with ram's horns. (9) During general

---

z   *Tamid.,* Chapter VII, *m.* 3.

a   *Raschius ad Succa,* Chapter V, *m.* 5.

b   See the *divin. Psalmod.* of the Cardinal Johannes Bona, Chapter 16, § 17.5.

c   Book IV, Chapter 9. [Presumably Josephus is meant.]

d   Matthew 6:2. [Luther speaks of having trombones sounded (*"lassen vor dir posaunen"*), whereas the King James translation mentions trumpets instead ("sound a trumpet").]

e   *Sanhedrin* and *Scharow,* fol. 36, *Kidrasch,* Chapter IV.

f   *Lund. Iud. s.,* Chapter V.

g   *Diodor. sic.,* Book VI.

calamities and wretched times. (10) During a rebellion. (11) For the victory of Gideon, [when] three hundred Israelites played trombones simultaneously.[h]

As time went on, trumpet playing became known to other peoples as well, such as the Greeks, Romans, Gauls or Celts, and finally—even though rather late—to the Germans. **Orichondas** brought it to Greece, and the [above-]mentioned **Tyrzaeus** *(Dyrtäus)* [took it] from the Athenians to the Spartans. The latter used it: (1) to call the community together, as **Propertius** says: *buccina cogebat, priscos ad verba quirites*; (2) to give the sign of war to the people, as **Virgil** says: *bella dat signum rauca Aventum buccina*; (3) at public services and sacrifices, and in particular to honor the well-known idol **Moloch**, [before whom] they would sing and play trumpets, partly to please the people and partly to muffle the murderous screaming of the burning children; (4) to propitiate the gods, as is shown by **Specerus**, quoting from ancient writers. Formerly, instead of [trumpets], fifes and flutes were used in war (as **Thyrcydides** and **Halicamassus** teach us).

The use of the trumpet by the old Greek peoples, in war as well as at the Olympic games and on other occasions, can be surmised from various accounts. Under the leadership of the great **Alexander**, the ancient Macedonians attacked the enemy army and the first cities to the sound of trumpets.[i] **Homer** relates that trumpets were used at the siege of Troy. One can learn about this [use of these instruments] particularly [by reading] the ingenious poem on the so-called War of the Frogs and Mice, as well as [by reading] about various Greek trumpeters, such as **Agyrtes, Herodorus, Misenus, Olympus, Phrygius**, and **Stentor**, who especially distinguished themselves on that occasion, and [who] will be mentioned in a special chapter.

Through a certain sound on the trumpet (called otondism) the Pythian actors imitated the gnashing of teeth of the dragon as the god **Apollo** 19   slowly approached to fight him.[k]

It used to be the custom of the Greek emperor in Constantinople to have trumpets and military kettledrums *(Heerpaukken)* play in front of him whenever he, for instance, rode out of or through the city, with the intent of giving anyone an opportunity to bring forth his grievance or his needs before the monarch himself.[l]

The Greek trumpeters and kettledrummers must also have been held in great esteem,[m] since they had even at Constantinople certain *Comites buc-*

h   Judges 7:8, 16[, 20, 22].
i   See Curtius Rufus. [Altenburg writes *Trompen*, probably a misprint for *Trompeten*.]
k   Vossius, Book III, *Instit. poet.*, Chapter 13, *Poll. Onom.*, Book IV, Chapter 10.
l   See Dr. Scriver's *Seelenschatz*.
m   Bulengerus, *de imperio Rom.*, Book VIII, p. 677, lit. I.

cinatorum,[n] otherwise called *Comitiva,* whose office was [considered to be] higher than that of the tribunes.

Lipsius [o] relates that the most noble Romans also made use of the trumpet. He says: *tuba digniores tantum canere solebant,* for trumpeters and kettledrummers enjoyed special rights and privileges, and the solemn use of their instruments was indeed varied, but never low or base. They used them: (1) at public divine services, for which reason the trumpet was considered a sacred and exclusive instrument, and the trumpeter a noble musician or exclusive trumpeter; as **Suidas** says in the place cited in **Lipsius'** [work]: *tuba sacrum hoc instrumentum nam sacerdos utebantur tuba.* The sound of the trumpet was also used (2) at the emperor's table, [and] (3) by the army, as an instrument of war for diverse purposes, especially in the field. When the Roman emperors and generals wanted to give a speech to the army, it was publicly announced beforehand by the sound of trumpets and kettledrums. [These instruments were used] also when the [Romans] took a city by storm and razed the city walls. In the latter case they employed the coiled *(gekrümmten)* [trumpets], and in the former, the straight ones. The Roman army commanders also used to celebrate their victories with the sound of trumpets and kettledrums, as we know 20 from the accounts of **Athenaeus** and **Polybius**. [These instruments were also employed] (4) at the weddings of persons of high rank—**Bulengerus** says: *in nuptiis tubarum usu frequens*—and (5) at other solemnities.

In Rome, the festival of the trumpeters (*tubilustrium*) was celebrated solemnly every year, when, in the month of April (namely on the last day of the *quinquatriorum*), the trumpets used at the sacrifices were played publicly, usually at the sacrifice of a lamb.[p] On the 23rd of May, the trumpeters celebrated [this festival] themselves. The [trumpeters] celebrated in honor of **Vulcan**, the [public] in honor of **Minerva**, and this ceremony is said to have been introduced by **Palantius** of **Arcadia**.[q]

The heathen celebrated the feast of the goddess **Cybele** with trumpets and kettledrums.[r] [The name Cybele] signifies the earth, which sustains and nourishes everything.

According to their obscure ideas of the divine, they believed that the more important a god or goddess might be, all the more glorious must be the music with which their festivals were to be celebrated.

Finally, [trumpets] accompanied by flutes and the singing of dirges (*naenanias*) were used in time of mourning and at the burial of young persons of high rank. However, this [music] was not performed by trum-

---

n *Loc. cit.*
o *Ibid.,* Book IV, Chapter 24, p. 471; Book VI, Chapter 48, p. 597, lit. d.
p In Dr. Mayer's *unvergreiflichen Gedanken über die Kirchenmusik,* Chapter 2, p. 23, the 13th of March is indicated. See also Schöttgen's *Antiquitäten Lexicon.*
q *Neapol. ad Ovid. I ante c.*
r *Silius ital.,* Book XVII *et Ovid.,* Book III.

peters serving in the army and playing on silver trumpets, but rather by the so-called funeral fifers (*siticines*), who played larger trumpets of a poorer [quality of] metal. These [funeral fifers] were not regarded by the military trumpeters as being quite honorable, for which reason they never associated with them.[s] Even though the office of trumpeter or kettledrummer was already held in less esteem by the Romans than by the Hebrews, [trumpeters] in the army still enjoyed more honor and freedom than other [trumpeters].[t]

21   In those days our ancient Germans did not yet know anything about trumpets and kettledrums. In their place they employed horns of aurochs and buffalo. Since they blew very loudly and lustily, they are said to have made a terrible noise with [these instruments].[u]

However, since the Germans took on the customs and habits of other peoples, through the wars they fought with them, they also adopted trumpets and kettledrums.

[The playing of these instruments] had formerly been a tradition of the French, beginning with jousting-bouts and other solemnities.[v]

It is not my intention to enter into an extensive historical description, but rather to show briefly that wind instruments probably came into common use with us [Germans] some time after the introduction of the Christian religion. **Schubart** [w] mentions that the sound of the trumpet was heard in the old castle in **Bacherach** or **Staleck**, where the ancient Counts Palatine formerly resided in the days of **Charlemagne** (it now being called the Emperor's Seat *(Kaiser-Stuhl)* near Rheinsee); he writes expressly: "the trumpet was blown in [times of] distress, and four of the Rhenish princes, each in his own land, were able to hear it."

Their use in German jousting-bouts can be seen from **Fugger's** account.[x] He says, "When in the year 1495 **Maximilian I** fought with the French knight **Claudius of Berre** about a knightly imprisonment, they came together on the appointed day, neither uttering a word, and **when the trumpeters sounded for the third time**, they couched their lances and rode against each other," etc. Until that time, brethren-in-art were still striving to maintain their standing, differentiating themselves from other, common musicians and pipers, either by serving at princely courts as court servants (*Mini-*

22   *steriales principis*) belonging to the princely household (*corpus domini*) under the jurisdiction of the court marshal, or else by enlisting in the army as military servants. Therefore, it was regarded as a particular sign of favor that the Roman Emperor **Sigismund**, in the year 1426, gave the city of Augsburg the privilege of retaining city trumpeters, since other free Im-

---

s   *Aulii Gell.,* Book XX, Chapter 2.
t   Lips[ius], *de milit. rom.,* Book IV, Dialogue 10.
u   *Diod. Sicul.,* Book VII.
v   *Pistoris cil. I. dissert. V,* p. 105.
w   In his *Spicileg. antiq. pulat.,* p. 137.
x   In the *Ehren-Spiegel,* Book VI, Chapter 22.

perial cities still had to manage with tower musicians.[y] Afterwards, sundry Imperial cities received this Imperial Concession upon application. The Noble Council in Nuremberg [still] retains a number of city trumpeters who perform also in that city's orchestra.

Trumpeters and kettledrummers formerly served under the direct jurisdiction of the sovereigns.[z] This right was later lost, until the emperors **Karl V** and **Ferdinand I**, following various protests advanced by [the trumpeters], restored it through an Imperial Dispatch in 1528. The emperor **Ferdinand II** granted them a particular Imperial Privilege in 1623, in consideration not only of their mastery of the art, but also of their station. This privilege was further elucidated and confirmed in 1630, the most important aspects of which will be mentioned later.

y See Sprenger in *delineat. Stat. Imper.,* p. 443.
z Chancellor Ludwig in *Germ. princ.,* Book III, Chapter 4.

Chapter 3

On the Present-Day Usage,

Benefit, and Effect of the Trumpet

The present-day usage of this wind instrument has, as it were, a great similarity to that of former times.

The differences as well [as the similarities] are due to:

(1) the manner in which it is played,

(2) the number thereof,

(3) the occasions, and

23 (4) the personages performing. All these points shall be dealt with later.

The different kinds of sound, as shown above, were called **Sounding an Alarm** and **Blowing** *(Trommeten und Schlechtblasen)* by the Hebrews. With us they are called **field piece** [playing] (wherein principale playing is included) and **clarino playing**; consequently, the kinds *(Art und Weise)* of trumpet sound, **as with the ancients**, are **two-fold**. The former, Sounding an Alarm, may have had great similarity to our present-day field pieces, because we know that it was also a broken and modulated sound, although it was perhaps not expressed with such artifice as we are used to. Blowing, or the long sustaining of one tone, is not in use with us any more.

Our long, thrice-wound instruments have the advantage over those [of the ancients] in that we can produce various melodies on them in the high register through clarino playing. [This clarino playing is accomplished] by the help of the tones [produced] by several trumpets [playing] simultaneously, in six to eight parts. Each [trumpet] part has its [own] peculiarly alternating melody [and is in a particular register of the instrument. Such a trumpet choir] can be used in harmony with other instruments.

Clarino playing with one trumpet is called a **solo**, with two simultaneously a **bicinium**, with three a **tricinium**, with four a **quatricinium**, etc.

24

However, the field piece always retains its usual name, even if it is sounded by several [trumpets] at once. If, for example, in the garrison only a single trumpeter [plays], or [if] in the encampment in the field all the army [trumpeters] together play Retreat or another field piece, it is and remains the same field piece and does not receive any other name thereby.

According to the Roman Emperor's Imperial Privileges, trained trumpeters and kettledrummers are supposed to use their instruments only in public ceremonies and never in company with untrained [players], on penalty of a high fine.

This prohibition goes so far [as to say] that they are allowed neither to blow the trumpet nor to beat the kettledrums together with the city pipers, even in church. Nevertheless, they are free at any time to blow and play other instruments in company with [these pipers].[8]

On the Particular Use and Effect of the Trumpet

Although our present-day field and military music in general has its particular value, the martial trumpets and kettledrums, with their blaring and heroic sound, are more suited than any other [instrument] for both frightening the enemy and—with their lofty tones—making the cavalry daring and bold. **Schmidt** [a] expresses it this way:

[The trumpet] stimulates heroes, inflames [both] army and battle;
And when it sounds the March, they move daringly
Towards enemy, danger, and blood.

The well-known poet **Horace** [b] attributes to [the trumpets] an affection inducing to rage and fury. "And," he says, "the priests of the goddess Cybele, the Coribanthes, are not influenced or moved to fury so much by their sounding of trumpets and cymbals as man is by harmful rage."

In the eighteenth ode [he says]: "O God, avert from me your trumpets and kettledrums which induce cruel fury."

Since the trumpet, owing to the major triad which it possesses by nature, can also arouse joy and pleasure, it is also played at celebrations of **Bacchus** and **Venus**. **Horace**, in speaking of wine-drinking, once said:[c] "Why do

---

8   This article of the trumpeters' and kettledrummers' Privileges was often violated. (See below, pp. 46-48.) A survey of the musical literature shows that trumpets and kettledrums were often employed in church music. Playing in churches and from towers was the domain of the city pipers. Two of the most famous Leipzig city pipers who were trumpeters were Johann Christoph Pezel and Gottfried Reiche. Reiche played most of the important trumpet parts written by J. S. Bach.

a   In his *Theol. Mus.*, p. 283.
b   In Book I, Ode 16.
c   *Op. cit.* III, Ode 19.

they already cease playing on trumpets and trombones?"

Terrible and frightful is the sound of the trumpet, however, [for instance:] when it announces the approach of the enemy, when the enemy orders the handing over of a besieged city through a trumpeter, or when he captures it by storm to the din of the war trumpet. In the same way, the blowing [of a call] to arms makes a fearful impression upon a weaker corps, surprised and surrounded by a stronger one.

25 Through this unusual music, of which many have made use as a stratagem in old and modern times, important victories, too, have sometimes been won. When, in the Seven Years' War, in which I participated myself, an enemy corps of considerable size overran a smaller and weaker one in the darkness of night, with the intention of cutting it off, it was entirely driven back and put to flight by the oft-changing sound of the trumpet [coming] from different regions—[a sound] which made the enemy fear that reinforcements were approaching.

Finally, mention must here be made that the Emperor **Joseph II** pleased himself to introduce trumpets and kettledrums in 1744 in all the dragoon regiments also, which [example] was later followed by the King of Prussia and the Elector of Saxony. However, in more recent campaigns of the Prussians, the kettledrums were dispensed with in the entire cavalry.

Chapter 4

On the Advantages
of the Privileged Trumpeters
and Kettledrummers
in General

The name "trumpeter" is doubtlessly derived from the instrument he plays. For this reason we understand [the term] "trained trumpeter" [to mean] one who has learned [to play] the trumpet as a musical instrument of war and pomp according to the rules of art, and who practises [his art] after having been declared competent therein by a privileged Roman Imperial fellowship *(Cameradschaft)*. The same [stipulations] hold true for kettledrummers; for since the kettledrums provide the bass or the foundation of this heroic music, these artists, too, are so closely bound up with one another that they belong to a closed guild *(Zunft)* and [are of] equal rank.

Those brethren-in-art *(Kunstverwandte)* who live according to the Roman Imperial Privileges and who [have] studied their art with one of the [guild-members] are thereupon called "privileged" or "trained" ·and may be employed as such by a court or a regiment, [may] enter Imperial, royal, Electoral, or princely service, and [may] participate with their art in all 26 solemn state occasions, Imperial coronations, tournaments, and the like. Others, however, who [have] not learned this trade in the above-mentioned way and who are at a court or in an army outside of the Roman Empire, are simply called "untrained," and for that very reason are not tolerated among us.

The Difference[s] Between Them

[Brethren-in-art] are accordingly grouped into two major classes, namely,

court trumpeters or kettledrummers, and **field [trumpeters or kettledrum-mers]**. They could also be divided into several subsidiary categories because there are among them **guard, regional, city, ship, and other trumpeters**, whereof [see] further below.

On the Court Trumpeters

Such trumpeters and kettledrummers are not only at the court of the Roman Emperor in Vienna but also with most of the spiritual and secular Electors and other princes of the Empire, where their work is of various kinds. Mr. von **Seckendorf** considers them essential to princely pomp, for besides [the fact] that the sound of the trumpet stands out more solemnly and magnificently [than that of any other instrument] (especially in the open air), [it is also true that] a grand sovereign creates a great sensation if he can display one or two choirs of trumpeters and kettledrummers, [all] clothed in sumptuous livery, and [blowing] silver trumpets. On state occasions and days of rejoicing, [such an assemblage] can make the heart receptive to every affection through its persuasive music.

A sovereign may have ever so good an orchestra, venery, royal stables, and other such ministrations, [but] if he does not retain at least one choir of trumpeters and kettledrummers, there is, in my opinion, something lacking in the perfection of his household.

At the Electoral Saxon Court of Dresden there are eight trumpeters and one kettledrummer, and at the time of the king of Poland there were twelve [trumpeters] and two kettledrummers. The three spiritual Electors of Trier, Cologne, and Mayence, as well as the Bavarian Palatinate in Munich and Mannheim, no less than the sovereign courts of Cassel, Darmstadt, Anspach, formerly Würzburg, the Hague, Stuttgart, Brunswick, Weimar in Saxony, Gotha in Saxony, Schwarzburg, Sondershausen, and others, always had eight, and smaller courts four, court trumpeters and one kettledrummer.

27   The court of Berlin dismissed them in 1713 at the accession of the royal administration of **Friedrich Wilhelm I** for certain reasons of which they themselves were the cause. They are, however, replaced as the case demands with the royal *Garde du Corps* and *Gensd'armes*.

The four neighboring courts of Anhalt—Zerbst, Dessau, Coethen, and Bernberg—have likewise done away with them.

I shall be silent here about the trumpeters and kettledrummers at the courts and among the armies of other European powers such as St. Petersburg, Constantinople, Lisbon, Madrid, Versailles, London, Copenhagen, Stockholm, Warsaw, Naples, Turin, as well as at the princely courts of Italy, because they do not generally belong to our guild. I shall mention only that the positions of court trumpeters and kettledrummers are often bound up with other notable services of importance. Some of them fill the position of a court, chamber, or travelling quartermaster, which [positions] are often combined in smaller courts but [kept] separate in larger ones.

The duties [of such a quartermaster] usually consist in the following:

(1) To summon the emissaries to audience;
(2) To invite the same, as well as other dignitaries, to table;
(3) To regulate in advance the quarters of the royal household on journeys;
(4) To have supervision over the servants in livery, particularly at meal-times;
(5) To travel forth on important matters, for which purpose a saddle-horse is usually kept for them, as von **Seckendorf** mentions in his *Fürsten-staate.*

Other [trumpeters] are also employed in the orchestra and in chamber music [groups] and for this reason generally receive the name of chamber or concert trumpeters. At several smaller courts, some or most of them hold the position of a kitchen, cellar, hunting, or forestry clerk. At the court of the princely abbot of **Corvey,**[d] one also performed the services of court organist besides.

The duties of court trumpeters are quite varied, according to the nature of the foreign courts. **Berckenmeyer** writes in his *Antiquarius* that when the King of Portugal wishes to journey forth, he usually has [the fact] made known beforehand, by trumpets, in the streets through which he [wishes to] pass.

The **doge,** or sovereign of Venice, is always preceded by eight trumpeters clad in magnificent livery, and by a child holding a white flag in his hand.

Furthermore, war and peace are also announced at many great courts by the sound of trumpets and kettledrums. For example, in 1768 in [St.] Petersburg, the war against the Ottoman Gate [was so announced]. The election of the Roman Emperor, also, is always made known publicly with the sound of trumpets and kettledrums.

The remaining usual duties consist, for instance, in the following:

(1) Playing at table at noon and in the evening, a [duty] usually performed by one alone—in the manner of a field piece, with sharp tonguing—or else by all [the trumpeters] together, accompanied by the kettledrums, playing the usual processional fanfares *(Aufzüge).* Thereby each one [at court] may be directed [to go to table]. At the Saxon court of Weissenfels where I was brought up, this [playing at table] was per-formed daily by one who was on duty for that week, [and] on Sundays and holidays at the end of the church service [it was performed] by all together. The same [is true for] certain extraordinary [celebrations] as well, [such as] state occasions or solemnities. However, at most courts the court and chamber quartermaster is freed from this [obliga-

---

d Corvey on the Weser, not far from the small town of Höxter. [Altenburg spells it "Hexter."]

tion of playing at table] because of his many other duties (except when he is absolutely needed). Just so, the chamber or concert trumpeter is spared the weekly playing at table, because through the blaring he would spoil the delicate and subtle embouchure [needed] for clarino [playing]. So also are the [concert trumpeters] generally listed in a higher pay [category] than the others and are presumably distinguished [from them] by their uniform, or [they may] wear their own clothing, the same as other virtuosos.

(2) Making music when people of high rank come in procession to assembly.

(3) [Playing] at various solemnities, jousting-bouts, and tournaments.

29 (4) The playing of a bicinium, tricinium, or quatricinium during mealtimes by two, three, or four trumpeters together.

(5) Sounding and beating a flourish *(Touche)* at the drinking of toasts, [by trumpets and kettledrums together].

On the City Trumpeters

I have said above that in the year 1426 the free Imperial City of Augsburg first received from the Emperor **Sigismund** the liberty of retaining trumpeters. Afterwards, Nuremberg, Frankfurt-on-the-Main, Hamburg, Lübeck, and others [were given the same privilege]. These [trumpeters] are employed also as musicians in the local orchestras and receive up to 800 Lübeck marks, that is, nearly 300 Imperial thalers, as salary.

Regional Trumpeters and Kettledrummers

[Regional trumpeters and kettledrummers] are found in Lower Austrian patrimonial dominions, where they serve in certain districts and domains, belonging besides to the usual guild. [Both this designation "Regional Trumpeters and Kettledrummers,"] and the name "halberdier" *(Hadtschier)* I find in the signature on an old document, [dated] Vienna, 1706. One should also note that it is not easy for someone to accede to the position of court, city, or regional trumpeter if he has not previously served in the field as a military trumpeter—except [that] possibly the sheltered son of a court trumpeter [might be accepted] through his father's intercession.

The word **halberdier** is a very old term, and actually denotes the **Roman Imperial Mounted Bodyguard**; now, however, [it means] Guard trumpeter or kettledrummer. Now, just as every regiment of the Guards has an advantage over other regiments in respect to salary, uniform, and rank, it may also well be [the same] with the brethren-in-art, because they also have the first claim on vacant positions at court.

On the Field Trumpeters

A field trumpeter is actually one who has served with the cavalry in time of war and has participated in at least one campaign with expeditions and guard duty (and still better, has been dispatched to the enemy). [Until these requirements have been fulfilled,] according to their articles and prerogatives, no [trumpeter] at a court or in a regiment—not even a court and chamber quartermaster, or a concert and chamber trumpeter—is allowed to affix his signature with [the title of] field trumpeter or to take a pupil into apprenticeship. That is why [a trumpeter or kettledrummer at court] is called merely a "court trumpeter or kettledrummer," although he can also perform the duties of a court quartermaster or of a chamber and concert trumpeter without being a field trumpeter at the same time. [A trumpeter or kettledrummer] in a regiment is a mere "trumpeter" or "kettledrummer." The word "field" among them is to be regarded as a word of honor that their ancestors earned by offering up life and limb, upon which [fact] the Imperial Privileges are actually based.

With certain armies there are also **staff trumpeters**, who could better be called "state trumpeters," because they serve more for reasons of state than of necessity.

The duties of field trumpeters will be found hereafter in a special chapter on field pieces.

Particular Uses of the Signature

It is to be further noted that the eldest [trumpeters] in the two chief fellowships in Vienna and Dresden carry the title of Chief Court and Field Trumpeter (Obrist- oder Ober-Hof- und Feldtrompeter). Those in Vienna are merely Assessors of the Roman Emperor's Imperial Privileges, concerning which I have in my possession an old document dated Vienna, May 15, 1706, in which they assume that title in their signature. At the convocations for the assumption or release [of an apprentice to or from his articles], at which brethren-in-art from various courts and armies are present, they make use of the following order, according to their Privileges, in signing: first the pupil's master signs, whether he be a field trumpeter or a kettledrummer; he is followed by the Roman Imperial trumpeters and kettledrummers, they by the royal, Electoral, and princely brethren-in-art or those of an Imperial count, [and] they finally [by] the remaining field trumpeters with their kettledrummers. This very succession is also observed at the assumption or release of a kettledrummer, [with the difference,] however, that [the kettledrummers] have priority hereby. Thus they have agreed among themselves and assented to this order [of signing].

A **ship's trumpeter** is one (be he trained or not) who seeks his fortune on the high seas.

Chapter 5

On the Advantages
of the Trained Brethren-in-Art
in Particular

I. A chief advantage is the confirmation of their charters or Imperial Privileges, granted for 167 years under the Roman Emperors **Ferdinand II** in 1623 and 1630, **Ferdinand III** in 1653, **Joseph I** in 1706,[9] **Karl VI** in 1715, **Franz I** in 1747, and **Joseph II** in 1767.

[They were] confirmed as well [by] the Electors of Saxony, [who were also the] Archmarshals of the Holy Roman Empire, [namely by:] **Johann Georg I** in 1650, **Johann Georg II** at the time of the Imperial Vicarage in 1658, **Johann Georg III** in 1683, **Johann Georg IV** in 1692, the King of Poland and Elector of Saxony, **Friedrich August I** in 1709, **Friedrich August II** in 1734, and finally, by the presently reigning Elector, **Friedrich August III** in 1769 or 70.

II. It is no small advantage that the brethren-in-art have their own **protectorate** in Electoral Saxony, because of the office of Archmarshal connected with it. For that reason, other Electors and Imperial princes, in cases of dispute among their trumpeters, refer the matter to the judgment of the chief fellowship in Dresden; they also have their charters renewed and confirmed by both the Roman Emperor and the Elector of Saxony, after which [a] further [confirmation is] given by the remaining Electoral and Imperial princes only at the request of their court and field trumpeters. This chief jurisdiction extends not only to all court trumpeters and kettle-drummers at Electoral and Imperial courts, but also to all brethren-in-art in Imperial armies and assemblages, as well as in Imperial cities.

As a patronage, usually every two years, the Elector of Saxony has two

9 Altenburg writes "1760."

trumpet pupils (there may also be a kettledrummer among them) learn this art from one of the court trumpeters or kettledrummers, paying a hundred Imperial thalers premium from his treasury for each.

In the Imperial Privilege of the Roman Emperor the following words are written: "nevertheless shall this gracious Imperial confirmation and verification—given to you, the field trumpeters and kettledrummers, by our aforesaid dear uncle, the beloved Elector of Saxony, and his successors, as the high patrons and judges of the field trumpeters and kettledrummers —be without prejudice or detriment to your possessed rights and preroga- tives." 32

In the one from the King of Poland and Elector of Saxony it is stated: "[. . . that] all the brethren-in-art of the Holy Roman Empire [always] looked to it (namely, to Electoral Saxony) [for protection] and were con- tinually in the habit of manifesting themselves accordingly."

III. It is also surely to be regarded as an advantage that the archangel **Gabriel** is set over trumpeters, in preference to all other musicians, as a special patron, [because he is] one who both protects the Roman Imperial Residence [and] to whom, moreover, the trumpet is particularly dedicated. This is also mentioned in the Privilege renewed by the Roman Emperor **Joseph I** [10] in 1706, in the following words:

> that every trumpeter and kettledrummer shall have the obligation of paying one Imperial guilder into the treasury of the region to which he belongs, which the chief trumpeter in the field is obliged to collect and send in. From this [money], every quarter, a [service of] praise should be held for the living and their prosperity, and a requiem mass [should be] said for the deceased—in honor of the holy archangel Gabriel, as our patron at the Imperial Residence and at other great courts. [Such services should be held] whenever the occasion for devotion may possibly arise at Electoral and princely courts.

Indeed, for this very reason it is the custom to this day to set up an annual celebration to [the sound of] trumpets and kettledrums [e] in honor of this great patron of the Imperial Residence and of its art. Hence it also happens, I daresay, that the brethren-in-art of some courts and armies have wings on their uniforms, in order to indicate thereby that, just as the angel brought the annunciation to Mary, so shall the trumpeter with his instrument also announce war and peace. This is to be found listed in the Saxon Curiosity Cabinet, wherein at the same time sundry bits of information are given on the Trumpet Jubilee celebrated in Vienna in 1730, when just a hundred years had passed since the Roman Emperor **Ferdinand II** had granted them their first Privileges.

---

10 Altenburg writes, incorrectly, "Ferdinand II." This Emperor, however, issued the Privileges is 1623 for the first time and confirmed them in 1630. The para- graph which he quoted from the Privilege of Joseph I corresponds to the 21st article of the 1653 Privileges.

e See the second treatise of the *prüfende Gesellschaft* in Halle.

IV. It is also a sign of their esteem that this trade received the name of a noble, knightly art in the charters, just as it is explicitly included therein **that a trumpeter or kettledrummer is to be regarded as equal to an officer.** For this very reason they have the right to wear good ostrich feathers on their hats, as do those of knightly rank.

V. Great sovereigns and potentates, at the celebration of their nuptials, are accustomed to open the dance with trumpets and kettledrums,[f] as a rule.

VI. Thus it must finally redound to the great honor of the entire society of trumpeters and kettledrummers that great sovereigns have deigned this art worthy of being taught to them.

The Duke of Weimar, in Saxony, had himself released [from his articles of apprenticeship] in 1734 according to the Privileges, after having first given his demonstration of trumpet playing in the presence of both his own and some unfamiliar brethren-in-art summoned for the occasion. His teacher, the court and chamber quartermaster **Schiel**, received an apprentice's fee of 100 ducats in specie, and the assembled society consisted of 34 trumpeters and kettledrummers. It indeed goes without saying that there was, on that occasion, no lack of pomp or ceremony.

I would have appended his letters of assumption and release to my work if I had had any occasion of obtaining them. For lack of them, and in order to show my readers in some measure what is customary on such occasions, I am taking the liberty of annexing my own letters of assumption and release. [Here, first, is my letter of assumption:]

In the Name of the Holy Trinity, Amen.

Herewith it shall be known that I, **Johann Caspar Altenburg**, Princely Saxon Chamber, Court, and Field Trumpeter, out of paternal attention to teach my son, **Johann Ernst Altenburg**, the worthy and knightly trumpeters' art, and on the occasion of the release of another apprentice, namely **Johann Michael Wenck** from Brüheim, have received and accepted him into apprenticeship. Now because this is not only my just right by virtue of the Imperial Privileges of the most gracious Emperor, but also [this having been] fittingly read to all the presently assembled gentlemen —that is, court and field trumpeters and military kettledrummers—and their kind consent [having been] obtained to this my son's reception and acceptance into the worthy trumpeters' art, thus has the following letter of assumption concerning this been drawn up. Namely, in the first place: the aforesaid, my son, is to persevere as a pupil of the worthy trumpeters' art from this day forward for sixteen years, and shall not be released sooner.[11] In the next place, I exempt him from the usual apprentice's fees of a hundred Imperial thalers, he being in no case obligated to pay

---

f   See the Menuet included here in the Appendix [on p. 144].

11   Sixteen years was, of course, not the normal period of apprenticeship. At this moment, on August 1, 1736, Johann Ernst Altenburg was just over two years old. (He was born on June 15, 1734.) Sixteen years later, on April 14, 1752, two months before his eighteenth birthday, Altenburg was released from apprenticeship. See pp. 37-39.

any part of this [sum] to either his mother or to his brothers and sisters. From now on he shall, in the third place, faithfully love and serve God and also show me, as his father and master, all imaginable respect and love; just as he [shall] no less gladly serve other accomplished comrades, and attend to his lessons as well, and always comport himself befittingly towards God, his superiors, and our most graciously received Imperial Privileges. In the fourth place, he is to receive and expect from me completely honest instruction and a paternal education. Now, should I depart this life prematurely, according to God's will, it shall be left in the hands of, first, his mother (thereafter, a worthy fellowship), to have him brought fully to perfection and strengthened [by] another accomplished court and field trumpeter in return for a tolerable gratuity—all of this conscientiously [and] without risk. In proof of which this letter of assumption has been personally signed and sealed by me and by all presently invested court and field trumpeters and military kettledrummers. These done in **Weissenfels,** the 1st [day] of August in the year 1736.

(seal) **Johann Caspar Altenburg,**
Princely Saxon Chamber [Trumpeter], also, Court and Field Trumpeter, as master and father

(seal) **Ernst Friedrich Renisch,**
Princely Saxon Court and Field Trumpeter

(seal) **Johann Christian Günther,**
Princely Saxon Court and Field Trumpeter

(seal) **Christian August Nicolai,**
Princely Saxon Chamber, Court, and Field Trumpeter, as well as Confidential Chamber Servant

(seal) **Johann Heinrich Thalacker,**
Princely Saxon Court Kettledrummer

(seal) **Johann George Tannbardt,**
Princely Saxon Court Trumpeter

(seal) **Johann Rudolph Altenburg,**
Field Trumpeter

(seal) **Johann Elias Urlaub,**
Princely Saxon Court and Field Trumpeter

(seal) **Johann Nicolas Berstedt,**
Princely Saxon Court and Field Trumpeter

(seal) **Georg Friedrich Röbock,**
Princely Saxon Court and Field Trumpeter

(seal) **Andreas Reebss,**
Princely Saxon Chamber and Court Trumpeter

(seal) **Johann Friedrich Nicolai,**
Princely Saxon Court Trumpeter

(seal) **Michael Sommer Werth,**
Princely Saxon Court Trumpeter, also, Court and Travelling Quartermaster

(seal) **Christian Joseph Nicolai,**
Princely Saxon Court Trumpeter.

At the assumption [of his articles], for the sake of correctness, the following compacts and points are read to the pupil, which he must swear to live up to faithfully: 35

(1) No one shall be admitted to the noble, knightly art of trumpet playing who was not conceived in a chaste, pure marriage bed.

(2) No military kettledrummer or field trumpeter shall presume to take on an apprentice except after the elapsing of seven years, [following] his [own] training, and duly performed campaigns.

(3) Should a trumpeter who has not been in the field dare to contract an apprentice, he is by all means to be prohibited from [doing] so. Because of [his] violation of the most gracious Imperial and Royal Privileges, he must also utterly surrender his trumpet as a penalty, until [there has been] fulfillment of the matter and [the attainment of] due satisfaction.

(4) If a trumpeter should be contracted to a regiment and also participate in campaigns during his two years of apprenticeship, these [campaigns] are nevertheless to be declared null and void, [being valid] only from the moment in which he is released [from apprenticeship].

(5) No assumption [to] or release [from apprenticeship] shall be performed, unless three or four members of a trumpet corps [12] abide thereby.

(6) All those devoted to the noble, knightly art of trumpet playing shall not presume to instruct a pupil without levying [a fee] of one hundred thalers, half of which—or fifty thalers—is to be paid in cash at assumption, and the other fifty thalers at release.

(7) A master, after releasing an apprentice whom he has taught, is to wait two years before taking on a new apprentice.

(8) If during an apprenticeship the apprentice shall have completed a full year and his master should depart this life, then the remaining 50 thalers [which are due] are to be paid without a single contradiction, to friends of the master, or to whomever the master has otherwise empowered. On the other hand, those levying the remaining 50 thalers are authorized to provide the apprentice with the training so urgently necessary [to him], and with the release which is required at that point, without [any further] expenses pertaining thereto.

(9) In case the apprentice should die within this period (it already being more than a year), then the remaining fifty thalers are likewise to be paid to the master.

(10) If an apprentice should allow himself to be seduced by dissolute company during his period of training so that he deserts his apprenticeship, he is neither to be tolerated at court nor in the armies of friend or foe, in the face of his offense, even though he may already have attained perfection in the playing of field pieces. As far as [it is] possible to receive such [a person] once again, he shall be obliged to commence his apprenticeship anew. In any event, if he cannot be retained, the full apprentice's fee is nonetheless to be paid.

12 *Cammeraden.*

(11) Inasmuch as an apprentice also mingles with womenfolk and should [thereby] make one pregnant, whether or not a year [of apprenticeship] has elapsed, not only shall the one hundred thalers be lost, but he shall by no means ever again be admitted to the noble, knightly art of trumpet playing.

(12) An apprentice is also required to serve all accomplished court and field trumpeters, as well as military kettledrummers, during [the period of] his training.

(13) No apprentice shall presume to associate with city pipers or horn players, much less teach them the field pieces; nor [shall he] use his trumpet at the beer-bench or at other peasants' revels, but rather [reserve his art] for emperors, kings, princes, counts, and sovereigns, as well as [for] all distinguished military officials.

After all this has been read to the above-mentioned apprentice, N, and he has agreed to abide firmly by the same, this letter of assumption is signed and sealed personally [by way of] increased ratification by Mr. N and other persons present, such as field trumpeters and military kettledrummers of the worthy regiment N. Thus done in N on the 21st [day] of June, 1714.

(seal) N, Cavalry Captain	(seal) [N,] Field Trumpeter, as master
(seal) N, Lieutenant	(seal) [N,] Field Trumpeter
(seal) N, Standard-Bearer	(seal) [N,] Military Field Kettledrummer
	(Feldheerpaukker)

Now, since each master has received his pupil into apprenticeship, he is therefore required to release him [from his articles] after the fixed period of training with good deportment and conduct. No one else may presume to [release him] without [the master's] assent and authorization, on penalty of 50 thalers fine.

As soon as the fellowship—which has been invited [to determine the apprentice's readiness for release]—has gathered, the pupil is introduced and judged according to the investigation of his deportment, manners, and aptitude; then he must first play the 5 field pieces as the chief demonstration [of his skill, and] also show that he possesses capabilities in clarino playing.[g]

Once he has accomplished this, he is made valiant by a slap on the cheek and given the dagger through which he becomes his own master. His teacher then presents him with his letter of release, personally signed and sealed by every one of the assembled fellowship, and each one wishes him good fortune on his acceptance into [the] art.

---

g If the pupil is skilled on several instruments, as is today considered necessary in many places, both the master and the pupil will have more glory and honor therefrom.

My own letter of release reads thus:

I, **Johann Caspar Altenburg**, having formerly served as Court Quarter-master as well as Chamber, Court, and Field Trumpeter to my most gracious lord and sovereign—the late Most Serene Lord and Sovereign, Lord **Johann Adolph**, Duke of Saxony, Juliers, Cleve, and Berg, also of Engern and Westphalia, Landgrave of Thuringia, Margrave of Meissen, also of Upper and Lower Lusatia, Princely Count of Henneberg, Count of the Mark, Ravensburg, Barby, and Hanau, Lord of Ravenstein, &c.; Knight of the Royal Polish Order of the Great White Eagle, also of the Royal Great British Order of the Blue Garter and of the Military Order of St. Henry; General Field Marshal of His Royal Highness of Poland and of the Serene Elector of Saxony, as well as General Field Master of Ordnance of the Emperor and of the Holy Roman Empire, also Colonel of an Electoral Foot Regiment, &c.—hereby proclaim to each and every one, of whatever rank, nobility, or office he may be, in particular to those devoted or related to the worthy, knightly field trumpeters' art, besides acknowledging my debt and [offering my] most willing services, that I accepted my son of a second marriage, **Johann Ernst Altenburg**, into apprenticeship to learn the worthy and knightly art of trumpet playing on the 1st [day] of August in the year 1736, in return for one hundred Imperial thalers apprentice's fees (from which, however, I exempted him, through paternal might and power, also through the most graciously granted concession of our most gracious Privileges), as stated in [his] letter of assumption, in the presence of many accomplished court and field trumpeters. Since he has not only proven himself in the years of his ap-prenticeship [to be] honest, loyal, devout, and obliging, but has also passed [his examination] on this day with his demonstration, in the presence of the undersigned court and field trumpeters as well as military kettledrummers, in such a way that they all had particular pleasure [in hearing it], the afore-mentioned **Johann Ernst Altenburg**, a pupil of mine until now, has thus been released from his apprenticeship and thereupon declared and acknowledged to be an accomplished trumpeter. [This re-lease is given,] however, with this express reservation: that the several-times-mentioned **Johann Ernst Altenburg** shall not have the power to receive, accept, or in any way promote a pupil, unless—according to the custom among trumpeters—he has participated in a proper campaign and has presented credible attestations to his deportment within seven years from [the date of] this letter of release received from me. For this reason, hereby and by virtue of this [letter], each and every one, of whatever rank, nobility, or office he may be, is petitioned by my due and most indebted desire and request, not only to give full credit to this [letter], but also to render full favor and beneficial attention to the oft-mentioned **Johann Ernst Altenburg**, allowing him to come into full enjoyment of this letter of release issued by me because of his honorable life and conduct. He will recognize this with the most indebted and obedient thanks, and I am most ready and willing to be indebted in return to anyone according to his rank. In augmented witness [thereof], not only I alone as father and master, but also the present [members of the trumpet corps], person-ally signed their names and imprinted their usual seals. Thus done in Weissenfels, the 14th [day] of April, in the one thousand seven hundred

38

fifty-second year after the birth of our only Redeemer and Savior, Jesus Christ.

(seal) **Johann Caspar Altenburg,**
Princely Saxon Chamber [Trumpeter], also Court and Field Trumpeter, as master and father

(seal) **Johann Heinrich Heinrich,**
Field Trumpeter

(seal) **Johann Christoph Altenburg,**
Field Trumpeter

(seal) **Johann Friedrich Jahn,**
Field Trumpeter

(seal) **Christoph Ernst Heinrich,**
Trumpeter

(seal) **Christian Ernst Fettner,**
Princely Saxon Court and Field Trumpeter

(seal) **Johann Heinrich Thalacker,**
Princely Saxon Court Kettledrummer

(seal) **Johann Gottfried Walther,**
Royal Polish and Electoral Collector of Tribute *(Frohnschreiber)*

(seal) **Johann Michael Dentzler,**
Princely Saxon Court Kitchenmaster.

VII. The estate of a [deceased] trumpeter or kettledrummer is inherited either by his nearest relatives or it falls to the local treasury.[13]

VIII. To support travelling or poor invalid [trumpeters] and their widows, the praiseworthy custom has been initiated at most courts, according to the 12th article of the newer Imperial Privileges, of having everyone pay 1 Imperial thaler or one guilder to the treasury each quarter, in order to help the needy with some small offering after they have shown their discharge papers. Even though this treasury may be exhausted or, in the case of a regiment, nonexistent, [such needy trumpeters] nevertheless are helped by a common collection [taken up] by means of a circulating slip of paper. Thus a travelling [trumpeter] who cannot play publicly should report either to the eldest of each court or to the one who is in charge of the treasury.

On the Advantage[s]
of
German Trumpeters in Particular

As far as we know, Germany produces the most capable trumpeters; for that very reason they are generally esteemed abroad and receive better pay [there] than in their [native] country. They are sought [after] and promoted even at the most remote ends of Europe.

Thus in 1722, the then King of Portugal, **Christian II**, had twenty German trumpeters and two kettledrummers simultaneously accepted into

---

13   See Wildv., p. 33. [This footnote, by Altenburg, was included in the main text.]

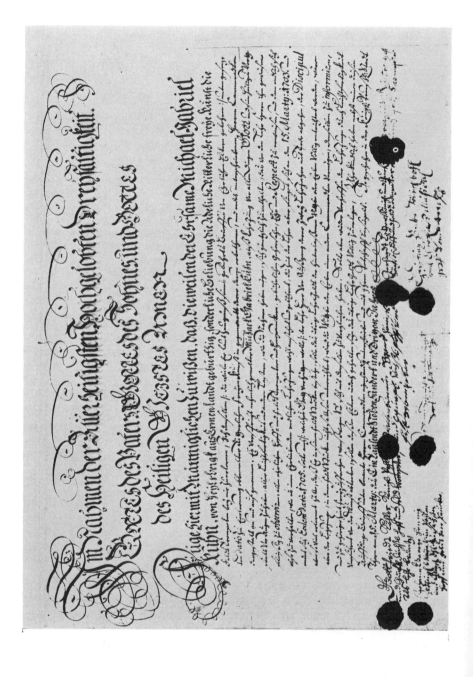

Notes for facing page.

An original letter of apprenticeship from 1703, from the collection of Ernst Buser (Binningen, Switzerland). Such documents are extremely rare. A number of letters of release have been preserved in various archives, but this is the only example of a letter of apprenticeship known to us at the moment. The German text of this document was printed in *Brass Bulletin* 3 (1972), p. 11. English translation:

In the Name of the Most Holy and Praised Trinity,
of God the Father, God the Son, and God the Holy Ghost, Amen.

I hereby make known to the public that the honorable **Michael Gabriel Kuhn**, born in Heilsberg in Ermenland, who desires me to initiate him into the noble, knightly, and free art of [playing the] field trumpet and whose birth certificate testifies that he was born of honest parents, has been received and accepted by me as a pupil of the above-mentioned knightly art, in the presence of the comrades who were asked to witness and sign this document.

The said **Michael Gabriel Kuhn** promises to keep in mind primarily **God** and His holy word, to refrain from wantonness and other vices, whatever their names may be, to be a diligent pupil to his teachers, to show due respect and obedience to all respectable court and field trumpeters and military kettledrummers, and, last, to behave in a proper manner as befits an upright, honor-loving apprentice.

The time of apprenticeship begins on the 15th [day] of March, 1703 and ends on the same date, 1705. If, however, the teacher should depart this life in the course of these two years—which God forbid—and the apprentice not be sufficiently instructed in the field pieces, then the widow or the heirs shall appoint another comrade to instruct him and to release him [from his articles] at the proper time, to which end the [widow or heirs] shall come to an agreement with [the new teacher].

Should, however—contrary to all expectation—the apprentice be tempted by wantonness to renounce the art, then his parents will nevertheless be required to pay the remaining apprenticeship fees.

In proof of which this letter of apprenticeship has been personally signed and sealed by myself and the comrades named below. Thus done in the Royal Prussian town of Thorn, on the 15th [day] of March, **in the year one thousand seven hundred and three.**

(seal)   Gottfried Köhler, Royal Polish and Electoral Saxon Court and Field Trumpeter, as Teacher

(seal)   Johann George Hennig, Court and Field Military Kettledrummer of His Royal Majesty in Poland and His Electoral Highness in Saxony

(seal)   Vallentinus Brand, Royal Electoral Saxon Court and Field Trumpeter

(seal)   Johann Heinrich Lindenbrecher[?], Court and Field Trumpeter

(seal)   Gerhardt Lotter, Royal Electoral Saxon Court and Field Trumpeter

(seal)   Georgius Richter, Court and Field Trumpeter

(seal)   Christian Breke[?], Royal Polish and Electoral Musical Court Trumpeter

his service through a certain German lieutenant under advantageous conditions, paying their travelling fees [h] and giving them gorgeous liveries and considerable pay.

40   # The Differences [Noted] in Services Abroad

In **Roman Imperial service** a field trumpeter is in one of the best positions—partly because of the honor bestowed upon him, partly because of the considerable pay. He receives 17 Imperial guilders *(Fl.)* monthly, along with a portion and a ration.[14] In return, he has to keep his own horse and procure his equipment. However, if his horse is shot dead in the field, it will be replaced.

In French service he receives 34 livres and 10 sous monthly and, furthermore, a gorgeous uniform. In time of war [he also receives] bread, meat, rice, and from the regiment, a horse.

The Roman Imperial Privileges are not in effect there; therefore, there are not only **trained** [trumpeters] but also city musicians *(Kunstpfeifer)* among them.

With the English a trumpeter receives 6 Dutch ducats monthly. Those of the blue guard are clad in scarlet uniforms with blue facings and short vests, both of which are trimmed with gold stripes. They have short silver trumpets with magnificent tassels, and silver kettledrums.

In Denmark the pay of a trumpeter is very low[:] 4 Imperial thalers and 3 shillings monthly, and poor uniforms. Moreover, if he gets a better uniform, with some few stripes (as is the case in most regiments), both are paid for out of his [own] pocket.

In Holland they receive uniforms of fine material, 18 Dutch guilders monthly, and [each one] rides his own horse.

I have not been able to gather trustworthy information on the remaining foreign services and will, therefore, move on to the situation of trumpeters in Germany.

On the Situation of the
Brethren-in-Art in the German Armies

In the Royal Prussian Army there is a slight deviation from the Roman Emperor's Imperial Privileges, in that city musicians or "art fifers" are

---

h   See Walt[her's] *musikal. Lexicon.*

14   See p. 56 for an explanation of what a ration is. By "portion," a food or fuel apportionment is meant.

taught the five field pieces for **one** or **two** years for 50 Imperial thalers of apprentice's fees and are thereafter admitted among the trumpeters who 41 earn their wages according to their period of service in the regiments. Their pay consists of 4 Imperial thalers and 16 groschen monthly. They go along on guard service, perform duties, and once they have become incapable [of fulfilling their obligations], they receive a civilian post.

The situation in which I find myself now will not permit me to say much about Electoral service.[15] I can, nevertheless, affirm that a trumpeter from Electoral Saxony observes strictly the Emperor's Imperial Privileges and [lays great stress] upon his honor bound up with them. The salary is 4 Imperial thalers and 16 groschen monthly.

When in 1753 a celebration was held near Ibigau and Dresden, all the brethren-in-art in the army handed over a note to the then commanding field marshal, the Count of **Rotowsky**, through the court trumpeters in Dresden, wherein they complained particularly about bad treatment at the hands of the officers. [This complaint] was so successful that a strict order was given immediately to all cavalry regiments, forbidding entirely such spiteful comportment and changing the various military punishments to simple arrest or a monetary fine. [It was] also [ordered that a trumpeter's] discharge, upon previous request, should not be denied him. A similar order is said to have been issued after the Seven Years' War as well.

The service of the trumpeters in Electoral Hanover has much in common with those of the Emperor's or of the Dutch [trumpeters], inasmuch as the [trumpeters] also ride their own horses. In return for this, however, they also receive double rations, and in wartime double portions as well. They also wear a handsome uniform. In the Seven Years' War their salary was [3 *Louis d'or* or] 15 Imperial thalers a month, the *Louis d'or* calculated at 5 Imperial thalers; in peacetime, however, it may well be less. I must further mention that they observe exactly the Emperor's Imperial Privileges and are for this reason highly respected.

Dispatches to the Enemy

This duty does not depend on the order of just any officer, but is rather arranged and ordered only by the colonel in the field, or [it may be also arranged] by the commander of a light corps. Because [the order can come only from these two officers], and because of the inherent danger to which one is at times exposed, I regard this [dispatching] as a field trumpeter's most important duty—especially since I can speak about this matter from 42 personal experience.

---

15   At that time, Altenburg was serving as organist in Bitterfeld.

Trumpeters from the free corps and hussars' corps are dispatched much more often than those from the heavy cavalry. Since the occasions for such are very diverse, however, the conventions pertaining thereto cannot be stated with absolute accuracy, it being instead left to each one to conduct himself properly, as the situation demands. One often receives several soldiers as cover, but sometimes not. Indeed, it also depends on whether one is being dispatched to an enemy encampment or into a besieged fortress, of which the latter is generally considered [to be] the most dangerous [duty of all].

I have also herewith the intention of informing young and inexperienced persons [about these dispatches], so that they will know in any case what they may expect from such a situation and how they should conduct themselves.

[When dispatched to the enemy,] the trumpeter is requested not to disclose his business to anyone, [neither on his own, nor] on the enemy's side. It is rather demanded of all subordinate officers, on their honor and duty, to see that a trumpeter's letters and messages proceed unopened and uninvestigated to the colonel in the field.[1] The trumpeter [who is delegated to carry a letter to the enemy] holds a distinctive position. In his dealings [with the enemy] he is intentionally accorded all the rights and privileges of higher ambassadors. Indeed, international law gives him in this case almost more freedom than other envoys, since the trumpeter—upon sounding a signal with his trumpet—is allowed to advance to the enemy army without a passport. A higher ambassador is in no case allowed [to proceed without a passport] under threat of [immediate] arrest.

When [the trumpeter] has received his clearance and instructions from the colonel in the field, he must [be careful to] put the messages entrusted to him in a safe place, so they cannot be soiled. [He must then] immediately begin his journey to the enemy lines, and continue [it] without delay.

Approaching the enemy, one should hold one's trumpet in readiness, which is necessary in any case because of the [possibility] of discovery by an enemy patrol while under way. As soon as the enemy picket is in sight, one should ride directly towards it, as close as [necessary for] the sound of the trumpet to be perceived. Then one stops short, giving with the trumpet, for example, a signal consisting of several so-called calls (Rüfe). If out of ignorance the picket gives a challenge, then one in any event, without paying any attention to [the challenge], gives another signal as an answer, until the enemy picket approaches and brings one—generally blindfolded, according to the customs of war—before the commanding officer. Into his and into no other hands are the dispatches to be immediately delivered.

Above all, one must be careful (1) not to let anything be noticed or

43

---

i   See the cavalry investiture (Reiterbestallung) of Speier, 1670, Article 64.

wheedled out of him concerning his army's possibly poor circumstances against the enemy; but rather (2) to pay heed as to how with good grace one might observe and bring back [information about] the enemy's position and other circumstances. If one does not receive any letter in return, one should (3) ask for a written statement that the dispatches have been properly delivered. Furthermore I would like to give everyone a bit of well-meant advice, that in such cases one should (4) conduct oneself soberly, moderately, and carefully, since one can otherwise easily run the risk of being shot dead.

Chapter 6

On the Decline and Misuse of the Art

The causes of the decline of the art were probably as follows:

(1) The separation [of the art] from the dignity of the priesthood.
(2) Misuse and ignorance [of the art] in German music in general.
(3) Wrongly mixing the terms "trumpeter" and "fifer."
(4) The barbarism and serfdom of that time in Germany.

It is certain that the priesthood—which with the Hebrews was associated with trumpet playing—was particularly honored by all peoples. It is just as certain that there was a diminution of [respect toward trumpet playing] as soon as these two functions were disconnected from each other (which, I assume, happened first with the Greeks). However, it must not yet have been of great importance, since we know that trumpeters, nevertheless, were still highly esteemed by the Greeks and the Romans, as I have already proved.

However, with the Germans, this art must have declined considerably, particularly in the Middle Ages *(in den mittlern Zeiten),* because neither an Imperial decree nor particular Privileges would otherwise have been needed for the restoration of their former esteem.

It is true that some worthless fellows tend to refer to just this Imperial decree of 1548, taking it as proof of the Germans' former contempt for trumpeters, and wanting to reproach them with it. On the other hand, the well-known Examining Society of Halle, in the aforementioned treatise of 1743, proved more than adequately that mere ignorance, misunderstanding, and false prejudice by the artisans of those times had caused this [loss of respect,] in that they did not know how to distinguish properly between

46

a trumpeter, skilled according to the rules of his art, and a common fifer or a minstrel *(Spielmann)*. They thought that trumpeters, since they lived either at court or with the army, were like serfs, [while] artisans, as citizens and defenders of the cities they had built and fortified, had been released from bondage and serfdom, through the intervention of the Roman Emperor **Heinrich I**, as early as the tenth century. On the other hand, people at court or soldiers [were considered to be] still in bondage. Finally, after serfdom had been gradually abolished entirely in Germany, all court servants also received total freedom.

Ignorance about music, on the part of listeners as well as of musicians themselves, has also contributed somewhat to this decline. For it is well known that not until the 14th century did the Frenchman **Jean de Murs** invent the various values of notes, setting them down as long and short, [while] they had all looked alike before and had been signified by mere dots. Even a hundred years ago, only very little was known about refined taste in music, although we had enough musical pieces. It was only at the end of the last century and the beginning of this one that [composers] started to imitate the Italians by writing melodious, tasteful pieces. Only since this time has music been allowed to enter the rooms of the great, who consider, value, and reward it as a noble pastime and a quiet private pleasure of cultured nations. We can therefore believe with absolute certainty that our German trumpeters of former times played nothing else but their field pieces, [and these] purely by ear, since one does not like to write them out anyway. One trumpeter would teach them to another for a small [gratuity], either voluntarily or perhaps, according to the bondage of that time, because he was urged to do so by his superior.

It is furthermore a certainty, that when a trade has once [started to] decline, it is generally taken up only by less gifted people. Thus there are some to be found probably even among the brethren-in-art, who themselves have not excelled—nor have they been able to, perhaps, because of the poor salary—and at the same time have misused their art. [For these reasons] the German sovereigns as well as the nobility have considered it superfluous to differentiate [among] such people.

Misuse of These Instruments

The prohibition of misuse of these instruments can be observed particularly in the eighth article of the Roman Imperial Privileges, where it is stated:

> No respectable trumpeter or military kettledrummer shall allow himself to be employed with his instrument otherwise than at divine service, or by the Emperor, Kings, Electors and Princes, Counts, Barons and noble

45

bodies of Knights, or otherwise by highly qualified persons. It shall be completely forbidden to serve on despicable occasions with trumpets or kettledrums, or also to wander about quite long at night in a dissolute manner in alleys [or] in wine- and beer-houses. Whoever should be [guilty of] such [a violation], should his offense become known, shall be punished.[16]

46   Special patents were also issued against all such abuses by His Serene Electoral Highness of Saxony, especially because of his office of Arch-marshal and Administrator of the Holy Roman Empire. Among these it is particularly noteworthy—because of all kinds of abuses [which had] crept in, affecting this art too closely—that the seventh point in particular of the Trumpeters' and Kettledrummers' Privileges was published [and confirmed] at that very time by the Most Highly Regarded Elector **J. George I** through an open patent.

Although, to be sure, the primary purpose [of these prohibitions] was the complete prevention of the misuse of these instruments, things must have later proceeded so much out of control that it became necessary, at the request of the Electoral Saxon brethren-in-art, to publish successively three reinforced mandates **Against the Unauthorized Playing of Trumpets and Military Kettledrums** in the years 1661, 1711, and 1736.[17] So that everyone may be properly informed, I wish to quote the most important [parts] therefrom. The first edict is based on the tenth point of the oft-mentioned Privileges, which reads as follows: [18]

> In the tenth place. Because trumpeters and kettledrummers perform solely for the Emperor, Kings, Electoral and Imperial Princes, Counts and Lords

16 These three sentences do not correspond to the eighth article of the 1653 Privileges; rather, the second and third sentences correspond to the eleventh article of these Privileges. (See footnotes 6 and 7 of the Introduction to this translation.) We therefore surmised that Altenburg had a later version of the Privileges at his disposal.
From Altenburg's list on page 31, we learn that the Privileges were confirmed at various times between 1623 and "1769 or 70" by the Emperors of the Holy Roman Empire and by the Electors of Saxony. On page 32, he quotes from a "Privilege renewed by the Roman Emperor Joseph I in 1706," and on page 39, he mentions the "newer Imperial Privileges." This "old document" (Altenburg, p. 29) from 1706 is, in fact, the version of the Privileges which was available to him.
The Privileges went through at least two thorough revisions after 1653—one in 1658 (see footnote 18) and another in 1706. Examination of microfilms of these three Privileges—films kindly made available by the instrument-collector, Mr. Ernst Buser—showed that Article 11 of the 1653 and 1658 versions had indeed been rewritten to become Article 8 of the 1706 version. It is from precisely this document that Altenburg quoted.
A comparative study of the Imperial Trumpeters' and Kettledrummers' Privileges, as they were revised through the years, would probably show that they were gradually changed in response to certain abuses which had crept in. Altenburg himself implies as much when he speaks of the mandates of 1661, 1711, and 1736 (p. 46).
17 Altenburg writes "1734."
18 It appears from Altenburg's text that in the first paragraph he quotes from the

of knightly rank, and similar persons of quality, and therefore do not belong in common to everybody, no respectable trumpeter or military kettledrummer, under threat of a penalty to be decided upon by the fellowship, shall perform with jugglers, tower watchmen, caretakers, or the like, [or] whatever they may otherwise be called, [even though they] may somehow be associated with the art, [for in so doing, the trumpeters will] thereby bring the art into great disrepute. Nor shall any comedians, jugglers, gamblers, tower watchmen, or even any city pipers *(Stadtpfeifer)* or minstrels, perform on trumpets or military kettledrums, outside of their stages, stands, or towers, or at weddings, baptisms, dances of rejoicing,[19] church festivals, or other similar convocations for counts, barons, nobles, townsmen or others; nor shall they use them—and certainly not trombones as if they were trumpets—for processional fanfares *(Aufzüge)*, dances, [or] blowing alarms. If any of these circumstances [should occur], the magistrates of each place, even without the trumpeters' request, shall refuse to tolerate such [actions] under penalty of a heavy fine, [thus] helping always to maintain and protect the trumpeters and military kettledrummers with this decree.

[Here follows the edict proper of 1661:]   47

By the grace of God, we, Johann George the Second, Duke of Saxony, Archmarshal and Elector of the Holy Roman Empire, &c.,

do hereby proclaim to everyone that our Chief Court and Field Trumpeter, and trusty and well-beloved **Hans Arnold**, has humbly brought suit in the name of our appointed court and field trumpeters and military kettledrummers, under presentation of the original patent. In our Electoral realm and territories far and wide, all kinds of abuses have arisen. Despite the severe penal mandates issued previously, not only tower watchmen, caretakers, jugglers, comedians, and gamblers [are sounding] the trumpet (as is tolerated of them on towers, in comedies, juggling games, and

tenth article of the Imperial Privileges, and that he quotes from the edict of 1661 in only the following two paragraphs. In reality, however, all three paragraphs are from the edict, a photocopy of which is in the possession of the translator. In its original form, the edict started with the titles of Johann George the Second, as quoted at the beginning of Altenburg's second paragraph; after some intervening material concerning the various confirmations of the Imperial Privileges and the complaint leading to the issuance of the edict itself, the edict quotes the tenth article of the Privileges, as found in Altenburg's first paragraph; the edict then concludes with the material found in Altenburg's second and third paragraphs.

If one compares the tenth article of the Imperial Privileges with its appearance here in the Altenburg treatise, one notices that the wording is considerably different. (See, for example, the English translation by Don Smithers, mentioned in footnote 7 of the Translator's Introduction.) Large parts have been changed. The reason is that Johann George the Second did not quote from the 1653 version of the Privileges, but rather from his own confirmation of them from the year 1658, in which the wording is quite different. The 1658 formulation found its way into Johann George's edict of 1661 and subsequently into Altenburg's book.

19 *Lobetänze.* According to Zedler's definition *(loc. cit.,* see Translator's Introduction), a *"Lob-Tantz* is when [*sic*] farmhands and maid-servants go home from the dance a great distance with one another, during the night, not without suspicion of incontinence. . ."

gambling stands),[20] but now all peasant musicians, besides the above-mentioned, have commenced to [do so] anywhere and everywhere it pleases them. [They sound the trumpet] especially at feasts, civic and peasant weddings, baptisms, annual fairs, church fairs, dances of rejoicing, and similar revels—indeed, even for persons of ill repute—in all rank intemperance and vexatious living (in these troubled times [21]). Some of them [sound] trombones as if they were trumpets, with the blowing of processional fanfares, marches, dances, and alarms, disturbing their fellows and thereby also grievously misusing the sound of the trumpet. [They do] so all the more because some of the delegated sub-magistrates of our territories have up until now not only overlooked [the actions] of such unauthorized persons, but have also employed them themselves in various places, thus introducing such abuse [themselves]. Since we were humbly requested to take under our most gracious protection the entire society of trumpeters and kettledrummers, both in our own and also—because of the office we hold of Imperial Marshal—in the neighboring Electoral and Princely territories, we are not able to refuse them, but wish on the contrary to adhere to the indicated Privilege and the mandate already issued on the 10th [day] of June, 1650.

[We] accordingly decree, to each and every one of our prelates, counts, and lords, &c., to whom this our patent might apply, that they [neither] allow, nor permit in the slightest, comedians, jugglers, gamblers, city pipers nor any city or peasant musician, whatever they are called, to play on trumpets or on trombones after the manner of a trumpet outside of their comedies, juggling games, gambling stands, and towers, nor at noble, civic, or peasant weddings, baptisms, annual fairs, church fairs, dances of rejoicing, or similar revels [respectively]; on [penalty of] a fine of a hundred Rhenish guilders of gold, which shall be levied uncompromisingly upon anyone offending against our mandate, half of which shall be delivered into our coffers, the other half, however, into the treasury of our appointed court and field trumpeters, in return for a receipt, in order that rank and vexatious living and prevailing abuses may finally be put to a stop. The above-mentioned superior and subordinate magistrates of our territories shall also punish appropriately the offenders and wrongdoers who have up until now employed the trumpet unlawfully, and shall order their trumpets to be taken away from them and handed over to our Chief Trumpeter. Thus is done my earnest will and intent. In testimony of which we have issued this patent with our own Electoral signature and printed seal. Thus done in Dresden on the 7th [day] of March, in the year 1661.

48

Johann George, Elector
(seal) **Wolf Siegfried von Lüttichau**
Christoph Schindler.

There further ensued a similar mandate in the year 1711. However,

---

20   After the words *"nicht nur,"* in the ninth line of p. 47, Altenburg omitted the following clause: *"die Trompeten (wie ihnen etwa dissfalls auff Thürmen / bey Commoedien / Gauckelspielen / und Glücks-Buden vergönnet/)"*. This clause corresponds to the following words in our translation: "the trumpet (as is tolerated of them on towers, in comedies, juggling games, and gambling stands)".

21   Altenburg writes *Leuten* ("people") instead of *Zeiten* ("times").

since the clauses of prohibition contained therein were variously interpreted because of [the] obscure and ambiguous manner of expression, and [since] the misuse of these instruments gained ground anew, a third mandate was finally promulgated in 1736 for the renewal and reinforcement of the prohibition previously issued in this matter, the alteration of which is as follows:

We Friedrich August, by the grace of God King of Poland, &c., Duke of Saxony, &c., Archmarshal and Elector of the Holy Roman Empire, &c., offer to each and every one of our prelates, counts, lords, those of knightly rank, officials, mayors and councilmen in cities, &c., our greeting, grace, and favorable will. [We] hereby submit to your knowledge the manner in which our chief court and field trumpeters, also court and military kettledrummers, have humbly lodged a complaint—in face of the Privileges possessed by them of old and confirmed from time to time, [and] in particular, however, [in face of] the mandates made known throughout the land in the years 1661 and 1711—because of unauthorized trumpet and military kettledrum playing by city pipers, also by city and peasant musicians, [which playing] has become all too common since that time in our Electoral realm and territories. [Such violators] have been protected by sub-magistrates through abuse and irregular interpretation of the clause inserted in 1711 in the latter mandate, and moreover, have even been encouraged by the approval of their courts *(Dicasteriorum)*. [We further submit to your knowledge the fact] that [the trumpeters and kettledrummers] befittingly request [us] to renew and reinforce the prohibition strictly expressed in the mandates alluded to, through the publication of a further universal order *(Generalis)* [drawn up] according to the wording [of the one] of the year 1661.

We have now graciously decided to defer to the supplicants' request, for the sake of putting a stop to the abuses which have arisen. According to the decrees previously issued in confirmation of their well-established rights and privileges, we hereby wish to renew the above-mentioned mandate from the year 1661 and, on the other hand, to restrict the above-mentioned clause [which was] inserted in the mandate of 1711. [The clause reads:]

[Trumpeters may not give] performances [or play] at meals, or at banquets with guests of honor, [unless these functions] are given by ministers, knights, officers, or by persons with a degree who are in our service or who otherwise fill a public office.

[This restriction] will have the effect that, on similar occasions, no one will be free to use any other than our court and field trumpeters and military kettledrummers, **when such can be acquired locally**, nor shall it be allowed to anyone at all in our service or in a public office to waive this [restriction, such waiver] rather [being permitted] only to our officials *(Diener)* and sub-magistrates who have a degree and hold the same rank as a high superior officer.

Our decree is accordingly promulgated to each and every one of our prelates, counts, and lords, those of knightly rank, and officials, &c.: that they manifest themselves in keeping with the mandate so announced and repeated, and [that they] not only observe [it] firmly and unerringly in respect to their own person, in order to avoid severe judgment and

49

certain punishment, but [that they] also forbid in particular the playing of dance [music], alarm, and processional fanfares on trumpets and other instruments—especially on horns after the manner of a trumpet and on the so-called invention trumpets *(Inventionstrompeten)*—in their own and their dependents' [areas of jurisdiction], except in the cases previously restricted or excepted; and [that they] in no manner allow anything to be undertaken against the oft-mentioned trumpeters' and kettledrummers' company, to their detriment or disadvantage. Rather [shall they] offer them our own proper protection and a helping hand against the violators and transgressors at all times; and if they should [take action] themselves or be petitioned in this matter again, after the application of the mandates of 1661 and 1711, they shall levy without delay the **one hundred Rhenish gold guilders fine** dictated therein from every transgressor, half of which is to be delivered into our coffers, the other half, however, to our appointed court and field trumpeters for their treasury, in return for a receipt; and [they shall] otherwise act fittingly. Thus shall my earnest will and intent be carried out. In testimony [thereof] the present mandate has been signed personally by us and ordered to be published under our printed chancellor's seal throughout the land. Thus done and given in Dresden, on the 17th [day] of December, 1736.

50

August Rex (seal)

Erasmus Leopold von Gersdorf.

Another important cause of the decline of the art is [the fact] that in some services, brethren-in-art are not properly appreciated [and] very capable people are not given special attention or rewarded. In military service one may be promoted only [to the rank of] **staff trumpeter**—one who in peacetime, however, is recruited by most of the German armies for mess duty; wherever he is still retained, he usually does not receive much more pay than any other trumpeter. Some armies do not have any [trumpeter] at all, I daresay; [k] or else he has to attend to the kettledrummer's duties as well. Positions for a trumpeter at court are nowadays rare and difficult to obtain and [are] a privilege befalling only the very few—partially because there are not so many courts at all today as there used to be, as I will presently show, and partially, too, because court trumpeters sometimes tend to push in their sons, to whom they have perchance taught their trade, whether or not they always possess the necessary capabilities thereunto. Consideration is generally shown in this matter to those in the mounted bodyguard as well.

51 The degree of advancement in similar court positions is either to that of Court, Chamber, or Travelling Quartermaster, or—where perhaps an orchestra or chamber music group exists—to service as a Chamber and Concert Trumpeter. The privilege and honor of Chief Court Trumpeter concerns only the eldest of the principal fellowships in the entire Roman Em-

---

k Here what Dr. Luther said is probably true: some of the nobility and the military think that they have saved my gracious lord three thousand guilders, while in the meantime perhaps thirty thousand guilders are squandered unnecessarily in return.

pire—namely, the Roman Imperial Court in Vienna and the Electoral Saxon Court in Dresden. Whether [these trumpeters] also receive a higher pay scale than other court trumpeters I can more easily guess at than state with certainty.

To be sure, it is also [evidence of] a considerable decline for the entire trumpeters' and kettledrummers' guild, that in the present century many eminent courts which previously flourished have gradually closed down. For those who are not well-read, I will touch upon the most important of these briefly, in order that everyone might better recognize the loss which the trade has thereby suffered. [I am especially aware of this], since I myself, as a child ten years of age,[22] witnessed this sad example at the Saxon Court of Weissenfels and—unfortunately!—still must bear the tragic consequences thereof to the present day.

I [shall] begin with the former Saxon courts: (1) Altenburg, (2) the old House of Gotha, (3) Eisenach, (4) Eisenberg, (5) Jena, (6) Merseburg, (7) Römhildt, (8) Weissenfels, and (9) Zeitz. Similarly, (10) Bayreuth, of Brandenburg, fell to Anspach, (11) Bamberg to Würzburg, and (12) Baden-Durlach to Baden-Baden. If we were to go back into the past century, several [more] of them could be found. Nevertheless, we wish to let matters rest as they are.

If I now calculate that there were eight court trumpeters and one kettledrummer at each of these twelve courts, together they amount to the number of 108 persons, [now unemployed there,] who formerly earned their livelihood.

If one were immediately to raise the objection to me that some smaller courts among these will hardly have kept eight court trumpeters, [I would like to state] that I have, however, not taken into consideration as well, the four courts of Anhalt already mentioned, and others, each of which, at least formerly, had a special choir of trumpeters and a kettledrummer. Nevertheless, I know positively that there really were this many at most of the above-mentioned Saxon courts, as well as at the others through which I travelled during the Seven Years' War.

In 1774 the Roman Emperor and several [other] powers introduced these   52
military instruments to the dragoon regiments as well.

It is also the symptom of further decline when some brethren-in-art themselves, out of greed, transgress various points of their Privileges. For half of the established apprentice's fees, [they] either teach others their art, or else, for a pittance, lend their names as masters to some who have never amounted to anything. In just this very way they wrongly increase the large number of trumpeters and kettledrummers, [a state] which runs completely counter to the true goal of the Privileges. The sentence contained

22 Actually, Altenburg was not ten, but twelve years of age when the court of Weissenfels was closed down in 1746. In his autobiography of 1769, Altenburg incorrectly gives 1736 as the year of his birth, instead of 1734. (See Arno Werner, *Musikpflege in Stadt und Kreis Bitterfeld,* Bitterfeld 1931.)

in the first article reads as follows: "No respectable trumpeter or military kettledrummer shall have the power to teach the art to more than one pupil at a time, not even to a brother or a friend, on penalty of 50 thalers fine—with the exception [that he may teach] his sons, should he have such."

In the second article the prohibition is written: "Nor shall anyone assume a pupil into apprenticeship for another master, on penalty of 20 thalers fine; but rather the master is obliged to instruct his own pupil in the best possible way and to bring [him] to perfection." All the same, some examples are known of one [trumpeter] instructing two or three pupils at the same time in the art, since he is only called the "master" by one and the "instructor" by the others, whom he must assume into and release from apprenticeship for other field trumpeters in return for a gratuity. This subtle device is a sign of unauthorized greed and selfishness.

[It is a] further [symptom of decline] when some brethren-in-art do not take proper care of themselves and do not conduct themselves befittingly before others, or do not see to it that they retain their regimental and company commanders as [their] patrons and protectors, at the same time always living on in the greatest ignorance of their art.

In this connection it is proper to mention the disunity which generally prevails in their doings, in that [trumpeters] do not stick together as they should; for when a realm is not at one with itself, it cannot survive.

[We should] further [mention] the cowardice [of some trumpeters who are afraid] to serve in foreign countries, particularly in times of war. [Participation in a campaign] is certainly expressly included in the Imperial Articles of their art, and it is to their advantage [to so participate], because [without doing so] they are not allowed [to assume the title of] field trumpeter [nor] to teach anyone else. I hereby see myself necessitated, although reluctantly, to reproach my own countrymen, the love of impartiality bidding me to do so.

I have it on good authority that at the beginning of the Seven Years' War, at a time when there were enough positions in all the armies, [a] certain [group of] nine Electoral Saxon trumpeters stopped at Linz in Austria, contenting themselves with troopers' wages as half-pay, [although] they easily could and should have served either their sovereign or his allies in the field. If this conduct were to have been based on the appearance of true devotion and love for their country, it would of course have been praiseworthy; however, since this was not so, it is therefore all the more reprehensible. These people simply belong to the category of that cowardly captain who ran from battle, crying to his trumpeter:

"See, see what kind of brave riders I have, how they can charge against the enemy and go bang! bang!"

"Yes," answered the trumpeter, "our riders are brave fellows and are not allowed to shrink from the most severe situation, but both of us are going to remain here, come h - - - or high water!" [1]

Finally, it also contributes to the decay of the art that the pay is so insignificant at some courts, as well as in many branches of the military, and [that] during service so few perquisites and gratuities can be expected, through which [lack], motivation is ultimately undermined.

Playing on New Year's Day is still one of the best [sources of extra income] with most armies; also, it is an old established custom that, when there is a death followed by a military burial, the trumpeter receives the dagger and boots, which usually lie on the coffin. Thus, when the time comes, one usually removes both from the coffin and gives them to the captain, who then releases them for a gratuity in keeping with the rank [of the deceased].

Conditions of Field Trumpeters in General 54

These [conditions] are now very diverse, according to the nature of the positions. Since I have essayed them myself, before, during, and after the passing of the Seven Years' War, and have seen and become acquainted with others as well, I wish briefly to undertake a reflection thereon based on experience.

Before applying myself to this [task,] I first wish to prefix [my remarks with] the eighth article contained in the Roman Imperial Privileges with respect [to conditions of the field trumpeters], in order that any impartial person may be able to pass judgment upon it more accurately; here it is:

> In the eighth [23] place. Every trumpeter or military kettledrummer should also behave so temperately, uprightly, honestly, and sincerely that he may be able to manage and perform his services willingly at all times, both for his master and mistress, and on [horseback] rides, guard duty, and other operations in the field. On the other hand, no colonel, cavalry captain, or commanding officer shall wilfully treat a trumpeter or military kettledrummer badly, as unfortunately was in vogue for some time. [He shall not] shame [him], despise [him], prescribe menial labor [for him] without good cause, nor throw him out of the service without pay, **but rather, as [has been] the custom as of old, treat him like an honorable officer and let him pass [for one].** Should one have served his year to the end and not want to remain with his lord, such a lord shall also owe him, along with the grant of an honorable discharge, his pay, [in the] correct [amount] and without deductions. If he does not receive it [as here specified], [his superiors shall] not be allowed to retain any trumpeter or kettledrummer until [the departing trumpeter has received] full satisfaction. Such [a] knightly art shall be protected by all praiseworthy courts in the name of the Imperial Privileges obtained [by the trumpeters and kettledrummers].

1   See Bär in *Ursus vulp.*, p. 27.
23   Altenburg writes "tenth."

Kaiserlicher Trompeter.

Engraving of an Imperial trumpeter, by Johann Christoph Weigel, c. 1700, from the translator's collection. Note the stripes on the uniform, and also the feathers in the hat—just as Altenburg describes them. (Photographic reproduction: University Library, Basel.)

I shall now deal with:
(1) the salary or pay,
(2) the uniform,
(3) the quarters,
(4) the horse, [and]
(5) the rank.

The pay varies, as I have shown above, and needs proper budgeting 55 if one is to stay within one's means in every situation.

The trumpeter must pay the cavalryman who feeds and grooms his horse and renews saddle and equipment, boots, &c., at least twelve groschen a month. Since the ordinary articles of [his] uniform are not sufficient, he must furthermore purchase his civil clothing, hat, boots, and fine linen himself, and make other purchases—partly because of the [necessary] order [of things], and partly [for reasons of] pomp—from [his salary]. A trumpeter shall and must live in grand style, especially when he is young and single.

The Elector of Saxony generally sees to it that a trumpet or kettledrum pupil (who, namely, studies at Electoral expense) receives six Imperial thalers living allowance; and when [one of them] is hired by a regiment, he receives 4 Imperial thalers and 12 or 16 groschen salary a month.

The uniform varies: In some armies they have fine cloth lined with chalon and trimmed with gold or silver stripes or bows, [and] stripes and good ostrich feathers on their hats, as formerly in the Luckner hussar corps. In other armies they wear dyed cock feathers, or I daresay no [feathers] at all, and simple ribbons like a non-commissioned officer. The jacket is made of heavy cloth with an inner lining of the same [material], and garnished with silk or velvet trimmings. However, in those positions where trumpeters are salaried with their uniform as well, they have the choice of clothing themselves with fine or heavy cloth; they all merely have to agree as to clothing.

I shall now deal with their **quarters**, of which there are two kinds, called [either] standing or billet quarters. I am speaking here merely of standing quarters in which a cavalry regiment is usually housed, either in cities or in the country.

In most places there is a service treasury from which all the officers as well as all the married men draw their lodging money, in order to [be able to] take a room and to purchase [for] themselves everything pertaining thereto. The trumpeter also must seek to use [this treasury].

The horse, together with the saddle and bridle, is either given by the 56 potentate in whose service one is engaged, or sometimes one rides one's own horse, receiving double rations—as for instance in the Roman Imperial Hanoverian and Dutch services. Each ration consists generally of five to six Imperial thalers monthly.

The rank of a trumpeter is not the same with all regiments; usually he is on the same level as a sergeant major.

Chapter 7

On Famous Trumpeters,
Past and Present

Since I already mentioned in the first chapter the trumpeters to whom the invention of the trumpet has formerly been attributed, although incorrectly, I consider it reasonable to help preserve the memory of deserving men who have particularly distinguished themselves in times past and present—partly as historical information for many, partly also as an example for others—that they may compete with each other to imitate them.

Here they follow in order:

(1) **Hemann,** who is said to have been the greatest trumpeter with the Hebrews.[m]

(2) **Achias,** a Greek trumpeter who was not only crowned three times in the well-known Olympic games, but to whom was also erected a column of honor because of his outstanding playing.

(3) **Aglais** of Alexandria, a daughter of Megaloclis, played a loud trumpet (and is also supposed to have been a voracious eater and drunkard).

57 (4) **Talthibius,** a trumpeter of Agamemnon.[n]

(5) **Herodot** or **Herodor,** a trumpeter from Megaris, rendered such good services to Demetrius Poliorcetes during the Trojan siege that the heavy war machine, Helepolis, was swiftly brought to the wall by the soldiers. Athenaeus relates that he was a very big man, and an even bigger glutton and drunkard.[o]

(6) **Misenus,** a Greek trumpeter of the brave Hector [p] in the Trojan War.

m See Kalkbrenner, *kurzer Abriss einer Geschichte der Tonkunst.*
n Agamemnon was the Mycenaean king who commanded the well-known siege of Troy for ten years.
o Book X, p. m. 414.
p Hector was a famous Trojan general.

58

After [Hector's] death he went to Aeneas [q] and is said to have been drowned there by the heathen god Triton because he had challenged the gods of the sea with his trumpet. The Neapolitan foothills (Ital. *Monte* or *Capo Miseno*) are said to be named after him because he was buried there.[r]

(7) **Stentor**, a famous Trojan trumpeter. He had such a strong, bellowing voice and such a healthy chest that he could speak and blow as powerfully as almost ten others [could do]. From him the musical adjective *Stentota* as well as the speaking-tube (*Tuba stentorea*) are said to have received their names.

Among the Germans [the following] have especially distinguished themselves in more recent times:

(1) **Hasert** (Johann), born in Bercka in 1680, studied music from early childhood and at seventeen [learned how] to make keyboard instruments *(Claviere)* and violins. In 1699 he learned the trumpeters' art at Eisenach, and in 1701 he joined the army, serving in nine successive campaigns at Brabant. During the winter he also attended the *Collegia musica,* [being] everywhere diligent. Thereupon in 1709 he 58 entered sovereign services as court trumpeter at Eisenach, where he constructed all kinds of good musical instruments.

(2) **Kegelmann** (Johann), a Prussian trumpeter, was equally good as theorist and composer, and, according to **Gessner's** information,[s] made himself particularly known through the printing of a music book at Augsburg under the title: *Concentus trium vocum, Ecclesiarum usui in Prussia praecipue accomodatos.*

(3) **Nicolai** (Christian August), Sovereign Saxon Chamber, Court, and Field Trumpeter, as well as private valet of the late Duke **Christian** of Weissenfels. [He] was held in high esteem at this court because of his ability, and was at the same time a favorite of the Duke. However, after the latter's death in 1738 he turned to the Prince of Thurn and Taxis, at whose court, still holding the same positions, he died at an advanced age in 1760. His son, who had formerly been court trumpeter at Anhalt-Zerbst, succeeded him.

(4) **Vogtländer** (Gabriel), a royal Danish court and field trumpeter, published in 1742 odes and lieder on the melodies of many Italian, French, English, and German composers, in folio.

(5) **Druschezsky** (George) [was] appointed Regional Kettledrummer at Linz in Austria, [and] edited pleasing *Partien* and suites (for various wind instruments) which are generally known in the Imperial Roman army. He is said to have been not only an able kettledrummer, but

---

q   Aeneas was a Trojan prince.
r   See Virgil's *Aeneid,* Book VI, Verses 232 ff.
s   *Partition univers.,* Book VII, *tit.* 7.

also to have been naturally gifted in musical composition and to have had considerable knowledge thereof.

(6) **Schreck** (J.) was formerly Court and Concert Trumpeter of Gotha in Saxony, and composed various pieces.

It is beyond all doubt that honor must be considered an essential part of an artist's reward. Children are obliged to render it to upright parents even after their death. Since I have here already made mention of other worthy brethren-in-art, I may indeed be allowed to say a few words about my late father also. Should there occur nothing noteworthy in this [discussion], at least the changes of the times and the decline of the trade will be learned hereby. I certainly hope that I will not be accused of self-glorification therefrom, since I could truly say more on this subject than I really do, because even now there are persons still alive who knew him personally.

(7) **Altenburg (Johann Caspar)** was born at Alach (a village near Erfurt) in 1689. Here he was sent to school and afterwards to music instruction by his parents. Since he took particular pleasure [in music] and had a natural gift [for it], he decided to learn the trumpeters' art. Therefore, with the permission of his parents, he set out in 1707 for Weissenfels to become an apprentice with the court trumpeter **Röbock**. Upon completion of his apprenticeship, the Saxon prince **Johann Adolph** (a brother of the reigning Duke **Johann George**) took him along into Hessian war service and engaged him in his own cavalry regiment which he commanded. Here for two years he witnessed the war in the Spanish Netherlands led against France, and the encounter at Malplaquet, which [even] for that time was exceedingly bloody. In 1711 he was accepted as court trumpeter by the reigning Duke of Weissenfels, **Johann George**, and was also provided by that prince with a special recommendation. In 1714 he married for the first time. Since this Duke passed away in the following year, [my father] was appointed Chamber Trumpeter in 1722 [t] by the succeeding Duke, **Christian**; also shortly afterwards in 1724 [u] with a raise in salary, he was drawn into the orchestra, which at that time was in high fashion. In

---

[t] Herewith [may the will be known] of the Most Serene Prince and Lord, Lord **Christian**, Duke of Saxony, Juliers, Cleve, and Berg, also of Engern and Westphalia, &c., [to the effect that] **Johann Caspar Altenburg**, [the servant of] Our Gracious Lord, &c., his Most Serene Highness, [has received] in grace the title of Chamber Trumpeter. Thereto the Most Highly Revered, Most Royal Highness has issued to him the present decree, [signed with] his own High signature and printed with his privy chamber and chancellor's seal. This done at his castle of residence, Neuaugustusburg in Weissenfels, on the 21st [day] of December in the year 1722.

(seal) **Christian**, Duke of Saxony (*H.z.S.*)

[u] We, [being] **Christian**—by the grace of God, Duke of Saxony, Juliers, Cleve, Berg, Engern, and Westphalia, Landgrave of Thuringia, Margrave of Meissen, also of Upper and Lower Lausatia, Sovereign Count of Henneberg, Count of the Mark, Ravensberg, and Barby, Lord of Ravenstein, &c.—proclaim and

1730 his wife died, with whom he had fathered five children. In 1731 he was asked, together with his colleague Nicolai, to play publicly for the King of Poland, **Friedrich August I**, in Leipzig. Here each one of them was offered a court position in the orchestra at 600 Imperial thalers salary by the conductor **Heinchen**.[24] However, they could not accept this offer because they could not obtain their leaves from the Duke. They also played at that time with the orchestra at the court of Berlin. In 1732 my late father, with permission of his superiors, travelled to the Thuringian region to visit his relatives there. On this occasion he took a look around at various German courts like [the one of] Gotha in Saxony; from there he travelled to Bayreuth, Nuremberg, Anspach, Stuttgart, Cassel, Brunswick, Wolfenbüttel, [and] Sondershausen in Swabia. He made another journey in 1733 to the cities [of] Hamburg, Schwerin, and Strelitz. At all of these aforementioned courts his playing was received with considerable applause. Not only were lavish gifts conferred on him at several [courts], but he was also offered a court position. At many courts his magnificent livery, obtained from his Duke, was greatly admired; and he has often spoken to me himself in the highest terms about the good reception and the courtesy paid to him. Although the preceding travel was actually the true purpose of this undertaking and the visit to his relatives only a pretext, he did not believe that anybody would know about it upon his return. However, since the Duke **Christian** had read

61

acknowledge that we have accepted our dear, faithful **Johann Caspar Altenburg** as our chamber trumpeter. As such, he shall be faithful and kind to us, and attend to our service with a sound horse, [shall] serve and promote our best interests to the best of his ability, and on the other hand shall fend off all scorn and prejudice. In particular, however, [he] shall carry out orders and instructions, both from us and from those to whom we shall refer him; [shall] let himself be employed as a chamber trumpeter in the court encampment in the field, on dispatches, in musical performances, or in any other way we may have need of him; [shall] be found properly mounted at all times, so that he can follow us on our journeys; and [shall] otherwise do and perform everything else fitting and proper for a faithful servant towards his lord. He has therefore dutifully promised and agreed to do [all this].

In return, and so that he may attend to this our service better and more assiduously, we wish to present him with 300 thalers yearly, beginning at Eastertime, free feed for his horse, and normal clothing. The 300 thalers are to be reckoned as follows: 220 thalers from our treasury entrusted to our Privy Councillor **Büttner**, and 80 thalers from our privy-purse, as a supplement for services [in] musical [performances]. In witness whereof we have signed [this document] personally and printed our Privy Chamber and Chancellor's Seal. Thus done at our castle of residence, Neuaugustusburg in Weissenfels, on the 17th [day] of July in the year 1724.

(seal) **Christian**, Duke of Saxony *(H.z.S.)*

24   Johann David Heinichen (1683-1729) led the famous Dresden orchestra from 1717 until his death. Since he died in 1729 and Johann Caspar Altenburg's trip to Leipzig is said to have taken place in 1731, there is some discrepancy of dates here.

about it in various newspapers, it was revealed. The Duke charged him with it, but instead of giving him a deserved rebuke, he raised his salary to 300 Imperial thalers yearly.

That same year he married for the second time; and in 1734 he was assigned—together with his colleague **Nicolai**, upon the gracious order of the Duke of Weimar—to be present at the previously mentioned [25] release [of the Duke] from his articles. Since they both played on that occasion, each one of them received 50 thalers as a present, and free board at the inn.

When later the Duke **Christian** died at Weissenfels in 1738 and was succeeded in reign by the third brother, **Johann Adolph**, this eminent orchestra was gradually given up, about which I shall say something later on. However, my late father was graciously named Court, Chamber, and Travelling Quartermaster with continuance of his salary. Since the Duke, as field marshal, also commanded the Electoral army, [my father's] main task in the well-known war and campaigns [of] 1744 and 1745 consisted in giving constant attention to the quarters of his Duke and his surrounding household. When finally in 1746, after the last Duke's death, the whole court ceased to be, the well-known Prime Minister Count of **Brühl** gave him the choice of either a court position in Dresden or a hundred thalers pension yearly. He preferred the latter to the former since he yearned for rest, and so spent his remaining years wholly in peace until he finally concluded his life in 1761 at the age of 73. He had had the grace of serving the princely court of Weissenfels, namely the last three reigning brothers, for 35 years. Within this time, through his intercession with the last-mentioned Duke, he brought my two older brothers into service as court trumpeters, and trained many good pupils.

His tone in clarino playing and the various modulations *(Modification)* thereof, which he was able to join skillfully with a singing, flowing character, his ease in the high and low [registers], his expression of the manifold ornaments *(Manieren)*, and his execution were, without false praise, something ingenuous and outstanding. Clarino playing was not at all difficult for him, and he was capable of delivering it so softly that it could scarcely be heard, yet each individual tone was clearly audible. He was generally much better in clarino playing than in the playing of field pieces or in the principale register, and therefore not every composition for trumpet was suitable for him. He valued particularly highly the pieces by the composers of that time, **Telemann, Förster, Linicke, Fasch,** and **Schreck.** In his musical instruction he was, as usual, more practical than theoretical, and in dealing with people he was very sociable, friendly, and obliging.

25   On p. 33.

But shouldn't other good people find their place here also? If their names had been sent to me by others, I would certainly have included them. In the meantime, nevertheless, I shall set down the:

List

according to their age and rank, of the brethren-in-art
at the Saxon court of Weissenfels,
[which] ceased to exist following the death of
Duke Johann Adolph in 1746

(1) **Johann Caspar Altenburg**, Chamber, Court, and Field Trumpeter, also Court, Chamber, and Travelling Quartermaster

(2) **Christoph Arnoldt**, High Princely Saxon Court and Field Trumpeter 63 and Court Quartermaster

(3) **Johann Christian Günther**, High Princely Saxon Court and Field Trumpeter, also Court Quartermaster

(4) **Andreas Krebs**, Princely Saxon Court and Chamber Trumpeter

(5) **Johann Rudolph Altenburg**, Princely Saxon Court and Field Trumpeter

(6) **Johann Friedrich Löffler**,^v Princely Saxon Court and Field Trumpeter

(7) **Christian Ernst Kettner**, Princely Saxon Court and Field Trumpeter

(8) **Johann Christoph Altenburg**, Princely Saxon Court and Field Trumpeter

(9) **Johann Heinrich Thalacker**, Princely Saxon Court Kettledrummer and Musician *(Musikus)*.

List

of the Roman Imperial Court Trumpeters in Vienna,
serving in that orchestra in 1766

(1) Ernst Bayer
(2) Franz Kreybig
(3) Andreas Hübler
(4) Neuhold [26]
(5) Koch
(6) Hofbauer.

v   The widowed Duchess chose him as her court trumpeter and court quartermaster, [and took] him to Langensaltz, where she had her dowager's estate and [where she later] died.

26 This is probably Peter Neuhold, who later became chief court trumpeter and the teacher of Anton Weidinger (1767-1852), releasing him from apprenticeship on September 18, 1785. Weidinger went on to be the greatest performer on the keyed trumpet, and it was for him that Haydn and Hummel wrote their trumpet concertos. See Reine Dahlqvist, *The Keyed Trumpet: Its Invention and History up to 1820 With Special Attention to Anton Weidinger* (North Easton, Mass., Robert King Music Co., 1974).

List

of the sundry brethren-in-art
at the
Electoral Court in Dresden [in] 1771

(1) **Johann Friedrich Schröter**, Chief Court Trumpeter *(Oberhoftrom-peter)*
(2) **Johann Christoph Schlegel**, Court and Field Trumpeter, assistant to (1)
(3) **Johann Gottlieb Frey**, Court and Field Trumpeter
(4) **Johann Wilhelm Kaditsch**, Court and Field Trumpeter
(5) **Johann Benjamin Wolf**, Court and Field Trumpeter
(6) **Johann Caspar Wolf**, Court and Field Trumpeter
(7) **George Andreas Wehlemann**, Court and Field Trumpeter
(8) **Christian Gottfried Mathäi**, Court and Field Trumpeter
(9) **Johann Christoph Hoffmann**, Court and Field Trumpeter
(10) **Johann Christian Salomon**, Court and Field Trumpeter
(11) **Johann Nicolai Geisse**, Court and Field Kettledrummer *(Feldheerpaukker)*; [he] is also a good mathematician.

Now, according to hearsay, **Mr. Kaditsch** is chief court trumpeter.

END OF THE FIRST PART

Practical Instruction

for

Learning to Play Trumpets and Kettledrums

Illustrated

with Rules and Examples

SECOND PART

"Battle Scene" —detail of an engraving by Jacques Courtois, called Bourguignon (1621-1675)

On the Various Sounds of the Trumpet,

the Intervals,

and the Relationships Thereof

Everyone who understands music will doubtless acknowledge that whoever takes up a musical instrument must, first of all, have an exact and true knowledge of its nature and characteristics, in order to master it properly.

Every art has two chief parts, namely: (1) a science (theory) and (2) the application thereof (practice). Therefore, these two parts—**knowledge and skill**—must be united, if one wishes to learn his art properly and thoroughly. Otherwise it cannot truthfully be said that one is [a] master of his art.

If one understands his art only theoretically—that is: if he knows everything pertaining to it but cannot perform on his instrument—[his knowledge] is of no more help to him than to others who only know how to criticize. On the other hand, if one is proficient [on his instrument] but knows nothing about its theoretical basis, he is today numbered among the lower musicians *(Handwerksmusikanten)*. When [a musician] has learned his art theoretically as well as practically, one can expect him to continue to make great progress in it.

Now, both [aspects] are much more necessary for our [instrument, the] trumpet, [than for other instruments—] partly because of its inherently missing and out-of-tune tones, but partly, too, because this instrument gives us more instruction in musical secrets than other, [more] refined instruments.

I shall attempt to set forth the most necessary and important [aspects 68 of trumpet playing] as clearly as possible.

The first [important consideration], which one must necessarily take into account before all others, is the variation in sound [obtainable on the trumpet], which I shall discuss from three points of view, namely:

(1) the sound in general,
(2) each sound [or tone] in particular, and
(3) the relationship of one [sound or tone] to another.

The Sound of This Instrument in General

[The sound of the trumpet] properly originates thus: two moving bodies collide with one another; [that is,] one [stream of] air is driven against another; or, [more specifically,] the air blown in [through the mouthpiece] circulates until [the air within] the entire metal tube is set into vibration thereby. This vibration is imparted [by the air in the tube] to the outside air, or pushes against it. Now, the stronger the air is set in motion and the more pronounced the vibrations, the louder the sound. Thus the trumpet does no more than determine the loudness of the sound in general. This same manner of sound production also takes place with the human voice, the organ, and all wind instruments, which are commonly called *pneumatica*.

Formation of the Sound

For a long time we have known how the sounds [or the tones] of this simple instrument are arranged, and how they progress one after another, although this [progression] was not [discovered] at once, but [only] gradually brought into proper order.

In the low [register] we have a series of seven euphonious sounds which can be blown on [the trumpet] without any great skill. Others lying between them are not easily produced, even though Nature placed [these seven sounds] there not in steps, but in leaps. The reason for this [difficulty] is that the very weak thrust of air required [to sound] the low tones can produce only the most perfect shaking (vibrations) of [the] air [column], for which reason it is not possible for the player to blow the several intermediate and
69 more difficult [sounds]. Depending on whether the afore-mentioned thrust of breath occurs through a larger or a smaller opening of the mouth, a slower or a faster movement of the air will arise from this, resulting in a lower or higher pitch. For the very reason that the high pitches make more vibrations, they sound louder and more penetrating to [one's] natural sense of hearing than the low [ones]. The higher we go, the more tones we also find which are somewhat more difficult and troublesome to produce. One can examine here what I have said about the formation of the sound. I see myself obliged to explain this somewhat more clearly.

I am well aware that trumpeters are in the habit of playing the low notes in field pieces and principale parts loudly and [are prone to] exaggeration for the sake of more fulness [of tone], but this is not a matter which concerns us here. As for the [tones] which lie between [the natural pitches], I believe that it is perhaps possible for some players with skilled embouchures to produce them—but with what effort! Probably no one is capable of sustaining such an artificial sound on a long note, several measures in length. To be sure, it can possibly take place with passing notes or [other] short notes; however, this is not a natural sound, but rather one induced by art.

These trumpet sounds can be notated in two ways, with or without using the staff.[a] Their range extends over four octaves, as is well known, depending on how high a [given player] can ascend.

On the staff, except for the two lowest tones, the [harmonic series of the trumpet] is written using the common French or violin clef at the beginning.

Improving the Staff

Since the trumpet has a series of tones in its low register different from that of other musical instruments, there seems nothing wrong in attempting to adapt it to a more compact staff.

g   c   e   g   c   d   e   f   g   a   b   c

---

a To designate [the various registers], many musical writers assign curious names to them like *Flattergrob, Grob,* and *Faulstimme,* etc., such as one comes across in Walther's *Lexicon* and Albrecht's *Anweisung zur Musik.* And if they were to be asked the reason for this, I doubt they would be able to give it. However, the notes can also be designated merely by using letters, a kind of notation which originates from the old German tabulature; for example:

great	unlined	one-line	two-line	three-line
C	c g	c̄ ē g	c̄ d̄ ē f̄ ḡ ā b̄	c̄̄ d̄̄ ē̄ &c.

[These correspond as follows to the designations used in our translation:
C   c   g   c′ e′ g′   c″d″e″f″g″a″b″   c‴d‴e‴ etc., *c′* being middle C.]

I would consider this staff to be better than the ordinary one for the following reasons: (1) because the frequent writing [of notes] above and below the staff and [the frequent use of] ledger lines would be eliminated, and (2) [because] no one could make a mistake thereby, since in the low register no other tones lie between [the ones notated]. [With this staff] only two lines would be needed for principale [parts], and only one for kettledrum notes. As for the latter, there is certainly an advantage to the many people who may not have supplied themselves with a staff-liner *(Rostral)*.

To be sure, I must confess that this is an unnecessary suggestion, but [it is] also one capable of realization. So far as I know, it has not yet occurred to anyone. Meanwhile, it could just be given a trial, the notation first being made known, then some bicinia and processional fanfares written out in it; and after it had been practised for a short time, soon [players] would become accustomed to it.

Each Sound in Particular

Because the proportions and relationships of the low tones are accurate, these tones are therefore perfectly in tune to the ear. They are generally [produced] in a blaring manner for playing field pieces, principale [parts], or at table, although we also use them softly on the second [part] or as accompaniment when two or more trumpets [are played] together. The low, or great *C,* however, is generally excluded, because it [has] a rather fluttering sound and is difficult to produce.

If we proceed further into the high register, several difficulties are found. One will note (1) in the one- and two-line octaves the out-of-tune tones which I call A♯ because they are too low for B♭;[b] (2) another out-of-tune tone between *e''* and *g''* which hovers, as it were, halfway between *f''* and *f♯''* but which gives neither pitch clearly and is thus to be termed a musical hybrid; (3) the *a''* which is also not in tune, but rather sounds a little too low—but this is not [a matter of] great importance.

Great artists can play much higher than this compass of four octaves, thereby not only bringing forth rather well the half tones *(semitonia)* which lie in the high register, but also, with a skilled embouchure and a good ear,

b The late Kirnberger, in his *Anweisung zum Clavierstimmen,* calls it *i* and numbers it among the consonances, observing that the augmented sixth has a rather pleasant [sound]. This is not the place for undertaking a closer investigation of this interval. Furthermore, such an investigation belongs in a textbook on theory.

improving the tones which are not naturally in tune. Thus they can also play solos, along with other instruments, in such other keys as G major and minor, and F major and minor.

However, if some venture to play semitones other than the aforementioned F♯ and A♯ in the two-line clarino octave, they are really exaggerating the art, [and such playing] falls into [the realm of] the ridiculous and the absurd, especially on long notes. One usually plays diatonically in this octave, although one can also play chromatically [in it], with respect to F♯ and A♯.

Diatonic and Chromatic

Many [people] are of the mistaken opinion that only that [music] can be diatonic, in which no sharps or flats precede the [individual] notes, therefore meaning that C major and A minor alone, and no other keys, are 72 diatonic. Actually it is possible to play both diatonically and chromatically in all keys. We know that every piece must have its own principal note, upon whose scale the entire melody rests. Now Nature has given every key a series of eight tones which follow each other in a precise order of steps which belong to that key alone and to no other. As long as one continues, sings, or plays [using] only these eight tones, one is playing melodies *(modulirt)* diatonically; but as soon as one leaves this series of [eight] tones and takes on one or two tones foreign to it, one modulates into another key. This exchange of key series or sequence of intervals is called chromatic modulation. Consequently F♯ major and E♭ minor, with six sharps or flats, are just as diatonic as C major and A minor.

If an F♯ is added, one thus modulates into G, because F♯ belongs to G major. If the high B♭ is added, one is at home in the key of F major, because [that is] where [B♭] belongs. An example will make the matter clearer:

The diatonic style is thus the most common and best [for trumpet music] and [it will] remain [so]. The reason for this may well be that the trumpet, because of its lack of half steps in the high register and whole steps in the low register, can produce a natural melody only in the diatonic genus, whereby the triad in the low register harmonizes only with [a diatonic melody].

If one were to ascend further and add F♯ and G, one would then have progressed and modulated chromatically.

73   We have probably become accustomed to writing the trumpet notes in C because this is the first and easiest key of all, [the one] which requires neither sharp nor flat signs. (Otherwise, other keys would serve just as well as this one, if [such a] practice were [now] introduced, or were ever to be introduced.) Thus—in [performing] a [piece of] music with other instruments, a trumpeter does not care in what key it is [written], or whether he is playing in C or C♯, for his part is always written in the key of C.[27]

Improving the Sounds Which Are Out of Tune

He who is endowed with a healthy sense of pitch will soon perceive that the aforementioned four sounds—*a♯'*, *f '*, *a' '*, *a♯' '*—are, to a greater or lesser extent, not perfectly in tune. Therefore one must necessarily try to correct them by using a skilled embouchure and a proper amount of exertion, if one wishes rightfully to deserve [to be called] artistic and expert.

I shall begin with the low *a♯['] or *b♭[']. It will be easily observed that this tone does not harmonize with any other, either above it or below it, and is therefore completely useless. However, when absolutely necessary, it is to some extent usable in the high register, but only when written as B♭, as proven by the previous example of the chromatic genus. It is also completely indispensable in unusual keys like F major and G minor. When making use of [this tone] one must attempt to raise its pitch, especially on long notes, because otherwise it would sound somewhat too low in relation to other [tones].

The tone found between *e['']* and *g['']* is not in tune either as *f''* or as *f♯''*, for it is somewhat too high for F, and too low for F♯. If, now, this [tone] is to produce its proper effect, one must necessarily let it fall, or lower it, for F; but for F♯ one must seek to drive it upwards or raise it.

27 It will be noted that Altenburg's remarks are valid only for Germany, broadly speaking. In France, Italy, and England, trumpet parts were notated in sounding pitch. Viennese Baroque composers were heavily influenced by the Italian style of composition and generally used the Italian trumpet notation.

The latter [situation] is also to be observed with $a^{[''']}$, in that that [tone], as well, sounds a bit too low.

I have already said that one must pay attention to the improvement [of these pitches] especially [in passages] with long notes, since at a high speed the player cannot accomplish [the improvement of these pitches], just as the listener would not notice [the out-of-tune tones] either.

Should, however, contrary to expectation, a given [player] regard this as a small matter, playing F instead of F♯ or B♭ instead of B, or vice versa, he would soon be convinced that he would [thereby] make even the very best melody discordant.

"Allein Gott in der Höh sey Ehr"

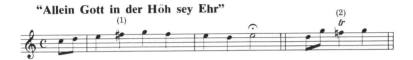

Everyone can easily see that at [figure] (1) it should be $f^{['']}$ rather than $f♯^{['']}$, and that at [figure] (2), on the other hand, it should be $f♯^{[''']}$ rather than $f^{[''']}$ because here the melody is being led into G major, which was not previously the case at [figure] (1).

As long as only one trumpeter alone is playing with other instruments, he can easily adapt [the pitch of his instrument] to theirs by ear. However, if several trumpets are played together, greater attentiveness is required to make sure that they are in tune in the high register, and also to the other instruments.

If the trumpet is played with a [well-]tempered instrument, especially the organ, still greater difficulties arise, which **Sorge** [c] discusses at great length in his treatise on tuning. This much is certain: that unless the trumpets and kettledrums drown out the organ, discord would very often be perceptible, especially if the wind instruments have not tuned up properly.

Sorge has designed a table showing which notes of the trumpet should be improved.

In another place he raises the question [as to] **"whether one should have doubts about introducing equal temperament in the organ because of the trumpets."** And he answers it thus: "Even if one were to adjust the pitches D—E, G—A of the organ so that their vibrations were in the ratio of 9:10, 12:13 as they are with the trumpet, the F♯—F and B♭—A♯, when played [on the trumpet], would still be out of tune with the organ. If [the trumpeter] can and must temper his naturally impure tones, he can also adjust the pure ones all the more easily, &c.["]. And here **Sorge** is absolutely right.

Mattheson has likewise gone to the unnecessary trouble of investigating precisely the relationship of the trumpet to other instruments according to

c   A former court and town organist in Lobenstein.

the monochord, thereby discussing the horn as well as the trumpet. However, these [relationships] are partly musical subtleties which may be differentiated from the point of view of the eye, but not of the ear, and which cannot be changed at all.

It follows from this [discussion] that a concert trumpeter must be particularly intent on tuning up his instrument accurately, as well as on improving the sounds which are out of tune by nature. [With regard to this matter,] the passage on the mute should be consulted.

All this might be enough for the mere practical musician, if one did not know that the eager, inquisitive theorist would already have a deep desire to become familiar with the tones of his instrument exactly according to their inner nature. If [the merely practical trumpeter] were to be asked by how much each of the impure sounds is too high or too low, he could not answer, much less determine anything definite.

Let us now consider **one sound in relation to the others**.

Intervals

In order to accomplish this [purpose], one must first become acquainted with the trumpet intervals, as well as with their relationships [one to the other] exactly [as they are]; and since these [intervals] follow one another in the most beautiful order on the trumpet, [the instrument] itself gives us right at hand the best opportunity [to make this kind of study].

It is therefore necessary to explain first what an interval actually is. **An interval** is a certain size of step [sic], or the distance between two different 76 sounds. From this [definition] it follows that two notes of the same pitch cannot form an interval, and thus I cannot say that either C and C, or D and D, are intervals. On the other hand, C C♯, C D, etc., are intervals. The word tone *(Ton)*, moreover, is usually understood to designate a precise interval—namely, when one progresses from one sound *(Klang)* to another.

These intervals are always counted off from the lower tone, that is, from the key-tone *(Grundton)*, according to the usual degrees and steps, are numbered, and are designated in the following way:

C	D	E	F	G	A	B	C
1	2	3	4	5	6	7	8
Prime or Key-tone	Second	Third	Fourth	Fifth	Sixth	Seventh	Octave

One can see from this [diagram] that D is a second away from C, E a third, etc., and although I have used C as the basis here, these intervals can nevertheless be counted off from all the other notes, as is customary in continuo [playing].

On the staff they appear in the following form:

These intervals can be regarded in different ways, namely according to time or space. [When regarded as to time,] the intervals are those in which two or more different tones follow one another, for which only one trumpet is needed. [Regarded as to space,] however, the intervals would be performed on two trumpets [playing] simultaneously. The continuo player divides [intervals] further into consonant and dissonant, major and minor, diminished and augmented, a classification which, however, does not concern us here.

Now in order to become familiar exactly with the different sizes, similarities, and relationships [of the intervals], and to determine them more precisely, Art and Nature have brought mathematical resources—namely, numbers [d] and [the] lines [of the staff]—to the aid of the inquiring mind. Therefore the experienced, theoretical trumpeter must also have some knowledge of the concept of the numbers of the harmonic [series], and the art of [their] measurement, if he indeed wishes to bring his art to true perfection. The [numbers] satisfy the understanding and determine the sizes and relationships [of the intervals] most precisely, while the [lines of the staff] make them visible and audible.   77

Relationships

According to **Mattheson's** description, a ratio *(Verhalt)* is that condition demonstrated by two given ends, or as **Spiess** says, [it is] the comparison of two different quantities.

If one wishes to compare one number or line with another, this [comparison] must be necessarily based on an equal or on an unequal ratio. In the former case, in which the ratio is equal, as in the unison, no further classification is necessary. In the latter case, however, there are many kinds [of ratios], of which we use only three for our purposes. [These are] the

---

d   Another series of numbers, however, are those numbers of steps[, 1-8,] indicating merely the outward number of the [eight] degree[s of the scale]; and still another are the proportional numbers, which penetrate to the innermost nature of the matter [and] with which we are concerned here.

pure or multiple, the *proportio superparticularis (übertheilige Verhalt)*, and the *ratio superpartiens (übertheilende Verhalt)*.

[A pure or multiple ratio] is [obtained] when a large line, string, or number, in comparison with a smaller one, contains [this smaller one] exactly two, three, or more times without any remainder, as for example:

1:2, 1:4, the single and double octave,[e]

1:3, 1:6, the double and triple fifth.

Here belong all the [ratios] which result in unisons.

78   The *proportio superparticularis* is [obtained] when a larger number or line, in comparison with a smaller one, contains the [smaller] plus a certain remainder, which is a precise subdivision of the whole. In this [category] belong [the following]:

2:3	3:4	4:5	5:6
Fifth	Fourth	Major third	Minor third

8:9	9:10	
Major whole tone	Minor whole tone,	etc.

The *ratio superpartiens* is [obtained] when the larger number or line contains the smaller one plus several additional parts of it, for example:

3:5	5:8	8:15	5:9
Major sixth	Minor sixth	Major seventh	Minor seventh, etc.

It is wonderful [to see] how Nature has already placed most of the intervals in this simple, natural instrument, the trumpet. Whoever wishes to convince himself of this [placement] needs only to write out the trumpet notes as they sound and set numbers above or below them [according to] their natural order. Then the [relationships] will appear naturally, for example:

The Relationships of the Trumpet Intervals

1	2	3	4	5	6	7	8	9	10	11	12	13	14	15	16
C	c	g	c'	e'	g'	$a\sharp'$	c''	d''	e''	f''	g''	a''	$a\sharp''$	b''	c''' &c.

e   The ratio one to two results in an octave, for example c', c''; one to four the double octave, once again as high, for example c', c'''. Whoever wishes to have more instruction in this [matter] is referred to **Marpurg's** *Anfangsgründe der theoretischen Musik,* or to **Sorge's** *Anweisung zur Rationalrechnung.* For him who does not want to enter into difficult calculations, **Türk's** *Anweisung zum Generalbassspielen* is chiefly to be recommended. It contains a very clear explanation of the above and several of the following relationships on pages 15-17.

These intervals are either consonant or dissonant, just as the relationships themselves are different. If one wishes to know the exact ratio [of a given interval], let him look up the numbers of the notes which outline the interval and they will show it very clearly to him, namely:

(1) Consonant [Intervals]

1:2 is the ratio of the octave   *C-c,*
2:3 is the ratio of the fifth   *c-g,*
3:4 is the ratio of the fourth   *g-c*[']*,*
4:5 is the ratio of the major third   *c'-e',*
5:6 is the ratio of the minor third   *e'-g',*
3:5 is the ratio of the major sixth   *g-e',*
5:8 is the ratio of the minor sixth   *e'-c' '.*

Everyone will see that the numerator of the preceding [ratio] always be-   79
comes the denominator of the following one.[28]

(2) Dissonant [Intervals]

8:9   is the ratio of the major whole tone   *c''-d'',*
9:10 is the ratio of the minor whole tone   *d''-e'',*
5:9   is the ratio of the minor seventh   *e'-d'',*
8:15 is the ratio of the major seventh   *c''-b'',*
15:16 is the ratio of the major semitone   *b''-c' ' ',*
24:25 is the ratio of the minor semitone   *g' ' '-g♯' ' '.*

In all we thus have thirteen relationships of the intervals, seven consonant and six dissonant, and one can see hereby at once to which type each belongs.

It will here seem strange to many that the relationships of the numbers 7, 11, 13, and 14 were not taken into consideration. This is because they are completely impure in relation to other [notes]. Just as the seventh number is incompatible with any other except 14, so does the note A♯ harmonize badly with tones above and below it, and except when compared with the higher A♯, it produces nothing but disharmonious intervals. For example:

With C it makes an almost augmented sixth   4 : 7
                                              c' a♯'.

With E it makes an almost augmented fourth   5 : 7
                                              e' a♯'.

With G it makes an almost augmented second   6 : 7
                                              g' a♯'.

28   Except for the ratios 5:6—3:5.

If one calculates these, it will be found that the first is too small by the ratio 35:36, the second by 63:64, and the third likewise by 35:36. The case is exactly the same with the high A♯, which falls under the number 14.

Although the [notes] falling under the numbers 11 and 13 also sound disharmonious, they are nevertheless somewhat more bearable. In the high register, moreover, there are still more [intervals] which get smaller and smaller, and which are, however, not altogether pure, especially those which fall under the numbers 17, 19, 21, 22, 23, etc. For this reason these, too, must be improved by artifice.

Now just as these relationships proliferate themselves in their natural order, they double themselves in the high octave, such as 1:2, 2:4, 4:8. One can perceive hereby that the tremblings of the air or the vibrations of strings stand in the same relationship as the tones themselves, only in reverse—namely, as they are described to the ear. When I say that the octave *c:C* has the relationship 2:1, [I mean also that] the vibrations are in the ratio of 1:2, and the same [is true] for all the remaining ones. This can be demonstrated in the following manner:

Note	C	c	c′	c″	c‴
Foot-tone	8	4	2	1	½
Vibration	½	1	2	4	8

The foot-tone here means the length of the trumpet, or of the whole string, and the lower numbers indicate the tremblings or vibrations of the air.

[In addition to] the [three] types of relationships [which I have already described]—the multiple, *proportio superparticularis,* and *ratio superpartiens* —there are still others such as the arithmetical and geometric, those involving similarities in height or depth, and others; but since these do not belong to my aims, I will pass over them completely.

[Concerning these others] one should consult **Sorge**, *Anleitung zur Rationalrechnung &c.* and **Marpurg's** *Anfangsgründe &c.*

Chapter 9

On the Mouthpiece, Tuning Bits or Shanks, Crooks, and the Mute[29]

The Mouthpiece

Next to the trumpet itself, the mouthpiece is undoubtedly the most important of the tools which the trumpeter needs to practise his art; through it the air is brought into the trumpet and set in vibration in such a way that the sound is brought forth. We have [mouthpieces made out] of silver, brass, tin, horn, and the like. Those out of brass are the most common because they are not expensive and yet are good and usable, and they do not produce the dull tone that [comes from] mouthpieces made of horn. Very much depends on the design and good construction of the mouthpiece, both as far as a good embouchure and the tone in general are concerned. Although it is difficult to determine anything definite on this [subject], I would still like to present some observations made from my own experience.

81

Herein we are concerned mainly with three parts [of the mouthpiece]; they are:

(1) **the upper rim,**
(2) **the inner cup, and**
(3) **the innermost opening, or the throat.**

The upper rim is either wide or narrow. A rim which is too wide hinders the embouchure somewhat, in that it reduces the freedom [of motion] of the lips and covers them too much. A rim which is too narrow, on the other hand, does not promote an accurate or enduring embouchure and tires the lips in a short time.

The so-called **cup** contributes much to the loudness and softness of the sound, according to whether it is deep or shallow, wide or narrow. With a deep, wide cup one can play louder, [and such a cup] provides good service

29 *Sordun (Sordin, Sourdin).*

mainly in the playing of field pieces or principale parts. On the other hand, a cup which is too shallow and narrow would not produce the proper loudness.

The inside opening [into the throat], according to its relative narrowness or width, influences the comparative highness and lowness of the sound. Since the air which is driven into a small opening remains compact, it is thus strong enough, on account of its elasticity, to set the resonant body into vibration at once and make it sound. On the other hand, if [the air] expands into a wider opening with less strength and pressure, it will then produce only the low tones.

82   **Bischof**, a former town trumpeter of Nuremberg, invented a special kind of mouthpiece which differed from the usual type in that on the inside of the outer rim there was another small, raised subsidiary rim, and inside the cup another tiny hole was to be found.[30] I used a mouthpiece of this kind myself, and acknowledge that it contributed very much to the improvement of my embouchure.

Many [players] use mouthpieces with a narrow bowl and a small throat in order to be able to ascend quite high. With such a mouthpiece, however, a pure clear sound in the high register [for clarino playing], as well as [a full sound] in the low register for heroic field piece and principale playing, is not quite possible. Therefore such mouthpieces are not advised either for clarino or principale players.

It generally is a prime rule that one should accustom oneself to only one particular mouthpiece, because the embouchure can be spoiled by frequent changes. Everyone must choose a mouthpiece suitable to the condition of his lips and the part which he plays. It would therefore be absurd for one with thick lips or for one who plays principale parts to want to select a mouthpiece with a narrow cup and a small opening, and so on. I will show beginners the external form and shape of my late father's mouthpiece, upon which he could, without forcing, reach high C, D and E. Here it is:

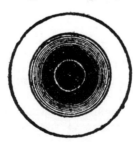

30   It is very difficult to tell what is meant here. "Still another tiny hole in the cup"— Could this be a device we still know today, whereby the tiny hole is opened to the outside when too much lip pressure is applied to the mouthpiece rim? Such mechanical devices, the aim of which is to help the player develop a light embouchure, have been invented and re-invented time and again.

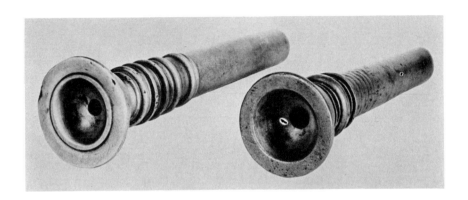

Left, trumpet mouthpiece, belonging to a German (?) trumpet dating from c. 1780—c. 1825, from the collection of Ernst Buser (Binningen, Switzerland). This may be the only mouthpiece in existence possessing "another small, raised subsidiary rim" "on the inside of the outer rim," as mentioned by Altenburg on p. 82. The "small, raised subsidiary rim" has the function of holding the player's lips firmly, enabling him to ascend particularly high. Such a mouthpiece, however, would hardly "contribute very much to the improvement of [one's] embouchure," as Altenburg writes rather diplomatically. On the contrary, such a mouthpiece gives a player the immediate feeling of being able to play very high, but would tend to weaken the embouchure if used regularly. Total length: 10.1 cm. Outside rim diameter: approx. 2.95 cm. Rim width: approx. .67 cm. Cup depth: .692 cm. Bore: 3.9 cm. **Right,** trumpet mouthpiece, late Baroque, from the translator's collection. Since it is difficult to play high on this mouthpiece, it was probably used for principale playing. Total length: 8.7 cm. Outside rim diameter: 2.8 cm. Rim width: .5 cm. Cup depth: .952 cm. Bore: 5.25 cm. (Photograph: University Library, Basel.)

I consider this kind of mouthpiece to be among the best. However, I do not recommend it as a general model, but rather [do I approve it] because many players who have used this kind could reach the high [tones] quite well with it.

83   It is also to be observed that in making [a mouthpiece] the upper rim be well turned down [on the lathe], so that it is not too sharp, because it would otherwise perhaps tire the lips, or even injure them.

Tuning Bits and Crooks

The so-called **shanks** [or tuning bits] are straight little brass tubes which lower the pitch of the trumpet. If one puts several of them onto one another, the pitch will be still lower. Since the trumpet would be uncomfortable to hold if the tuning bit were too long, the longest ones are wound in the shape of a circle or bent into a curve, for which reason they are also called **crooks** (*Krummbogen*). However, it is known from experience that with the use of the latter the trumpet is somewhat harder to blow. This [difficulty] is no doubt caused by the frequent curves through which the air is driven.

The tuning bits and crooks are as varied as they are necessary and useful, differing partly in their size and length, partly, too, according to their use and effect. There are some [tuning bits] which lower the pitch of the instrument by a whole tone, a half tone, a quarter tone, or I daresay even less, while [there are] some [crooks] which lower it by two tones, a tone and a half, or a whole tone.

I have already mentioned that the trumpet, according to its nature, can modulate only diatonically, and can cadence only as far away as G major, on account of the high F♯. [It follows] therefore [that] the player must adjust his trumpet so that it harmonizes exactly with the tonality of the piece to be played, if he wishes to play in tune with other instruments at the same time.

The trumpeter who does not play concertos or sonatas can do without the crooks if need be, and can get by with some short tuning bits for tuning with other trumpets. On the other hand, the chamber or concert trumpeter must by all means have the types mentioned above.

84   As is well known, our musical instruments do not all have the same pitch, for the reason that an exact foot-rule has not yet been introduced.[f] I will therefore try to give a short description [of the various pitches now in use].

f   The Royal French Academy in Paris has invented and defined such a foot-rule.

Choir and Chamber Pitch

In order to play in tune it is necessary for everyone to know the difference between choir and chamber pitch. It actually consists therein: that choir pitch, as far as the sound is concerned, is a whole tone higher than chamber pitch. [31] Thus the former sounds fresher and more thrilling, but it is somewhat troublesome for singers. [I might add that] organs as well as trombones &c. are usually in choir pitch.[32] However, it is known that the old organs are usually in a higher pitch than the new ones. On the other hand, chamber pitch sounds pleasanter and more serious and is also more suitable for voices and wind instruments, and therefore almost all musical instruments are adjusted to it. The matter can be represented approximately as follows:

What is in **chamber pitch**   C, c♯, D, E♭, E, F, f♯, G, a♭, A, B♭, b, &c.
is in **choir pitch**   B♭, b, C, d♭, D, E♭, E, F, g♭, G, a♭, A.

From this [outline] everyone can see that, as far as the pitch level is concerned, B♭ in choir pitch sounds the same as C in chamber pitch, C in choir pitch the same as D in chamber pitch, D♭ in choir pitch the same as E♭ in chamber pitch, etc. It will also be noted that the usual keys are printed in large type, the unusual ones in small type.

Tuning

Because nowadays chamber pitch has become almost universally established, both within the church and without (that is, in the chamber), all tuning is thus regarded [as having been done] according to chamber pitch except when certain chorales and songs of praise such as *Herr Gott, dich loben wir &c.* are sung with trumpets and kettledrums alone, without other musical instruments. In this instance only the trumpets and kettledrums are tuned to the organ, which is still usually tuned to choir pitch. However, in some places they have begun to introduce chamber-pitched organs. 85 Where there is a piano *(Flügel)*, the trumpet is tuned to it so that, for example, for a D trumpet, one asks to have the note D sounded [on the piano], which should sound like a C on the trumpet. It can thus be clearly

31 Altenburg is speaking about the situation during the entire 18th century, when choir pitch was a whole tone higher than chamber pitch, which in its turn was about a half tone lower than our present-day pitch of A = 440. See also footnote 5 (to p. 11).
32 In this respect it is striking that many cornetts now preserved in museum collections, for example in Brussels, are about a whole tone higher than our present-day pitch. Presumably the cornetts and trombones, which formed the church "orchestra" of the seventeenth and early eighteenth centuries, were tuned to the organs.

seen that there are about eight common keys, although several more of them might be possible.

If one wanted to play and be in tune in these [eight keys], one would also have to have eight trumpets of different sizes. However, so many are not really necessary, since by the addition of tuning bits and crooks a concert trumpeter needs only three trumpets (or at most four)—namely, the chamber-pitched D, F, and G trumpets. I have already discussed this matter in Chapter I, under the heading, The New Kind, First Class.

I will begin with the high keys. In order these would be:

(1) B♭ major. However, since such short trumpets do not exist, and moreover, because it would become painful and difficult for the player thereon, it is preferred that one play an octave lower in this key, using a long trumpet.

(2) A major. Here if one takes the short or G trumpet and inserts a mute, one will be in tune.

(3) G major. [Use] the above trumpet, also called the English [trumpet].

(4) F major. [Use] the field trumpet, otherwise called the French [trumpet].

(5) E major. Here one adds a tuning bit to the above trumpet which lowers [its pitch by] half a tone.

(6) E♭ major. A whole-tone crook is put onto the F trumpet.

(7) D major. [Use] the German chamber-pitched D trumpet, although many are also pitched in E♭.

(8) C major. A whole-tone crook is put onto the D trumpet.

86   For B♭ major, let one take a trumpet constructed especially for this [key], if he does not wish to put on a crook and tuning bits which together lower the pitch [of the D trumpet] by two whole tones.

I have said above that the crooks and tuning bits must be most accurately measured.

However, if the tuning [g] is still not accurate, one can easily assist oneself with very short tuning bits or with a little paper wound around the mouthpiece, so that the [mouthpiece] does not go in too deeply. It will also be [of] no small advantage [to the trumpeter] if his mouthpiece has been accurately turned out all the way around so that it goes into the trumpet to the necessary depth, because it is always easier to lower the pitch [of the trumpet] than to raise it. It should also be mentioned that there are various other pitches according to which instruments are fashioned in a few foreign places, such as the Roman, Venetian, and French pitch. However, these will not be considered here.

g   Many trumpeters, in tuning their trumpets, [ask to have] the third [degree] of the scale—such as the high e″—sounded, and [they] tune their trumpets to it. However, the third is not to be recommended for [tuning]. It would be much more accurate to employ the fifth, the octave, or the unison, because [with] these, it is easier to achieve unity. [The third in the harmonic series, is lower than that of the well-tempered system. For this reason, if the trumpet is tuned to the third, the rest of the instrument will be too sharp.]

The Mute[33]

The **mute** *(Surdun* or *Sordin)* takes its name from *surdus*: that is, weak or subdued. It is properly an instrument turned out of hard, firm wood which, it is true, makes no sound by itself; but when it is inserted underneath into the trumpet, it not only gives the trumpet a completely different, almost oboe-like tone, but it also raises it [in pitch] by a whole tone, if it is properly turned.

[I might add that] the **mute** must be a very ancient tool, since one can already read about a muted trumpet *(buccina surda)* in Juv[enal's] seventh Satire.[34]

There are different kinds of [mutes]. The first is equally narrow at both ends, the second is almost like a bell or a shawm at one of its ends, and the third kind has the shape of an oboe or clarinet towards its end. At the bottom [of this kind of mute there are] several small wooden rings which can be inserted or removed at will, [through the use of which] the sound can be made louder or softer. This has a singular effect when [one plays] with other instruments.[35]

The mute is properly used:

(1) When an army wishes to break camp silently, so that the enemy will not be aware [of its intent].
(2) At funerals and burials.
(3) To develop a good enduring embouchure through daily practice; and
(4) (With some mutes) to keep the tone from being so screeching; and also
(5) To bring [the trumpet] into tune with music in many keys therewith.

Mattheson mentions the mute on page 63 of the first edition of his *Organisten-Probe*, where he discusses the question of why [the mute] on the trumpet yields purely all the intervals in chamber-pitch E major but not in choir-pitch D major. Of course, this rise in pitch does not take place in the actual key, as one would like to think; for then it would have to be dissonant and would prove that C and D are not one and the same key.

---

33 *Surdun.* *(Sordin.)* Altenburg does not use the present-day expression *Dämpfer.*
34 Altenburg has misinterpreted the source, which speaks of a *"surda . . . bucina"* or a mute (i.e., silent) trumpet, not a muted one.
35 Concerning an entire collection of eighteen mutes from the eighteenth century preserved in the Historical Museum in Prague, see Jindřich Keller, "Stará trompetová dusítka" ["Old Trumpet Mutes"], in *Časopsis Národního Muzea Historické Muzeum,* Vol. 40, No. 1 (1971), pp. 25-31. There are two basic types of mute in the collection. One type (15 mutes) has the shape illustrated by Mersenne in *Harmonie universelle,* Livre Cinquiesme, p. 260. There are three of the other type, possessing a double corpus, one of which always differs slightly in measurements from the other so that a different pitch level may be attained when one or the other corpus, respectively, is inserted into the bell of the trumpet.

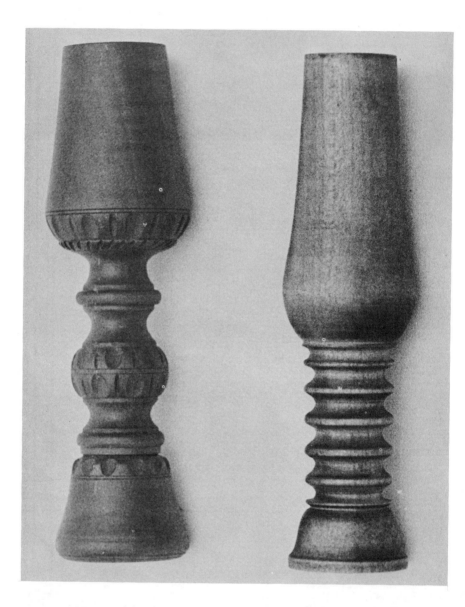

Two wooden Baroque trumpet mutes. The one on the left (15.1 cm high) presumably dates from the 17th century and is in the possession of the Historical Museum, Basel. An exact reproduction of this mute is now being made by Todd Barton (Ashland, Oregon) and it is available from The Brass Press. The one on the right (14.3 cm high) is presumably from the 18th century and is owned by Gerhard Stradner (Vienna). (Photograph: Christopher Brodersen, Sehmsdorf, West Germany.)

[The answer to his question is rather that] the trumpet, as an unalterable instrument, retains the proper relationships of C major, which are not the same as those of the key of D major, even with the rise [in pitch]. [It occurs also because] chamber-pitch E, but not choir-pitch D has the same diatonic relationships [as C]. Therefore [in E] it is perfectly in tune.[36]

---

36 This passage makes sense only when one realizes that Mattheson was not discussing today's system of equal temperament, but rather a specific kind of unequal temperament for the organ preserving the trumpet intervals in the keys of C and E. Altenburg furthermore does not quote Mattheson quite accurately—but this inaccuracy is of little importance.

Chapter 10

On the Heroic Field Pieces,[37]

Principale Playing,

and Playing at Table,

as Well as on So-called Tonguing

and Huffing[38]

What Sounding an Alarm and Blowing were to the Israelites, our present-day field pieces are [to us]. They are similarly used in the field for military actions. After trumpet playing had been introduced among other peoples, attempts were also gradually made to improve it and to bring it to an artistic form.

Our present-day field pieces are nothing more than an artistic variation on the major triad, placed by Nature in the low register of the trumpet. Since this [triad] sounds exalted and joyful by nature, the field pieces can also evoke a similar passion.

If one wishes to compare the former Sounding an Alarm and Blowing with our field pieces, one can assume that the former, an interrupted sound, was comparable to [our] 5 field pieces, while Blowing resembled the low posts [39] thereof.

Although the inventor [of the field pieces] cannot be stated with certainty, it can nevertheless be seen that he must have been an intelligent and talented man [h] to have derived such a beautiful variation and diversity from the six

---

37 A more accurate translation of *Feldstück* into modern English usage would be "military signal." However, the words "field piece" have been chosen instead because they are visually closer to the term employed by Altenburg and thus better preserve the character of the original.

38 *Haue.*

39 The term "post" used here (the correct singular and plural forms in German are *Posten*) refers to a section, or sections, of a field piece.

h Not completely founded in fact, my dear author! [It is] not [only] to be taken into account that an inventor does not always have to be an intelligent man;

low tones *c, g, c', e', g',* and *c' '.*

It is to be regretted that the old modulations [i] [of the field pieces] have gradually lost [any] resemblance [to their original form] through mutilation. Moreover, they have been so capriciously played that their true purpose and melodiousness have been obscured, especially in such field pieces as are played by many [trumpeters] together.

Of all the field pieces, none is more improperly played, by all armies, than the heroic trumpeters' march. It should be played more slowly for the heavy cavalry, in order to express the serious and heroic passions, and more briskly for the Hussars, a light cavalry.

This [very situation] moved the then chief court and field trumpeter, **Johann Christian Haas** [40] of Dresden, at the instigation and [because of] the complaint of the Muster-Inspector and General von **Rechenberg**, to set the march down in musical notation. He sent it, along with a written commentary, to all the cavalry regiments of the Electoral Saxon Army, with the command that they should play it just like the *Garde du Corps,* so that at the impending festival encampment at **Ibigau** a uniformity in the playing of the march might be observed. This order is still in effect today.

We Germans have 5 field pieces in all.

Of these, three—namely, the first, fourth, and fifth—are played alike except for the low posts,[k] in which they differ appreciably. Since each has its own purpose, character, and meaning, I will begin here with the first call.

I. *Boute-selle* or *Portés selles,* that is, bring up the saddle, [an expression which] is derived from Boots and Saddles. It contains three so-called calls *(Rüfe)* and the same number of high and low posts, and it usually [is sounded] two or three hours before riding out on horseback. The exact time for this call depends on the commander-in-chief. Its real meaning is the encouragement [of the troops].

II. *à Cheval,* to horse, or mount up. [When this call is sounded,] the cavalry must assemble and fall into line. In the encampment [this] usually [takes place] at the front, [while] in the garrison [the cavalry lines up] in front of the headquarters of the commander-in-chief. This field piece consists of five posts.

III. *Le Marche,* the march, which the French also call *Cavalquet* from *Caballus.* As soon as this is blown it is a signal to draw swords and to march off, although for the first a special command is usually given.

but it is also probable that this invention is not due to merely one person, but only gradually came to a certain state of perfection—if indeed this can be said about the field pieces.—Note of the corrector [of the 1795 edition].

i **Modulations** is incorrect here; the author would better and more correctly have said **"the first and oldest field pieces,"** which he presumably is speaking about.— Note of the corrector [of the 1795 edition]. [The two footnotes *h* and *i* were suppressed in the 1911 Dresden facsimile edition of the Altenburg treatise.]

40 *Hasen* (the accusative of *Haas* or, possibly, of *Hase*).

k They are thus named because they are played on the lowest tones *c* and *g.*

This call consists of four so-called posts and the breaking-off,[41] which is the usual signal to sheathe swords, and [it] can be played single or double.[42] See the **march** &c. [on p. 143]. The **breaking-off** of the march follows on p. 93.

IV. *La Retraite,* retreat. Its true character is one of calm, and [it] is usually played in the bivouac in the evening after sunset, as a sign that all is calm, still, and settled. The signal [to blow this call] is always given by a cannon shot. However, in the garrison, it usually takes place either before the main guard or before the quarters of the commander-in-chief. Like the first it contains three calls, three high and low posts.

V. *à l'Étendart,* to the cavalry colors or to the standard. This [call] means to assemble and line up. When the regiment has been charged by the enemy, it must, at this call, gather again at the standard and line up in order. It likewise consists of as many calls and posts as the first and fourth [field pieces].

The French have yet another [field piece] which they call *l'Assemblée*—that is, assembly. It is usually sounded a few hours after *boute-selle,* after which all are to assemble on foot, leading their horses by hand, but they are not [allowed] to mount up until *à cheval* is blown. This [order] was probably introduced to spare the horses.

A long time ago the so-called *Abtrupp* was also introduced in a certain army. This is played on the march home or on decampment. However, I pass over it here, since it does not interest us further.

91 **There now follow some more field pieces and pieces of rejoicing, such as:**

(1) *Alarme,* the blowing of alarm, an admonition that danger has arisen and one should take up weapons and move out. This is usually played with sharp tonguing.

(2) *Apell blasen* is the signal summoning the cavalry to retreat. **Fasch** in his *Ingen. Lexicon* lists other meanings thereto, usable at summonses, settlements, agreements with the enemy, and the like.

(3) *Ban,* that is, [to call attention] to a proclamation, announcement, or request.

(4) *Charge,* the signal to attack the enemy bravely. Here some play [a] march, others [an] alarm.

---

41 The *Abbruch* (Ital. *rotta*) meant a standard closing formula, or group of short formulae, in trumpet fanfares. It is mentioned in either German or Italian, in such diverse trumpeters' notebooks and methods as those of Thomsen (1598), Bendinelli (1614), and Fantini (1638). In this connection, see the editor's notes to the facsimile edition of Cesare Bendinelli's trumpet method, *Tutta l'arte della Trombetta,* appearing in the scholarly series of publications, *Documenta musicologica* (Kassel, Bärenreiter-Verlag, 1974). *Abbruch* has been translated as "breaking-off."

42 See Mersenne, *op. cit.,* p. 264, where the *Cavalquet* and the *double Cavalquet* are notated.

(5) *Fanfare* is usable on all days of celebration and state occasions and is usually played on trumpets and kettledrums together. It contains (a) the Intrada or *Intraitte*—that is, the introduction to a musical piece or a short prelude, which the trumpeters are accustomed to improvising before they play their instruments—[and] (b) *Tusch* (*Touche*), or flourish—[upon] the word or sign given to the trumpeters that they are to play, when noblemen drink toasts at table. This is the same as the preceding. Properly it is a short free fantasy consisting of nothing but a mixture of arpeggios and runs. Indeed it makes noise enough, but there is neither art nor order in it.[1]

(6) *Guet,* the watch, [is used] when [the watch] pulls up or is relieved. A march is used for this by the Electoral Saxon Army, and in the Prussian [army a piece] in the clarino register almost like a bicinium [is played].

(7) **Blowing at table** is performed by one court trumpeter alone, and is played like a field piece with sharp tonguing. However, the aforementioned announcement call *Ban* is [more] correctly [used], giving notice that persons of rank wish to get up and go to table.

(8) **The principale [part]** or **principale playing** is never performed by itself, but is actually the lowest part of four-part pieces usually called processional fanfares (*Aufzüge*), of which more will be said later. Thus the principale sometimes presents the bass, sometimes a middle part. The principale is probably so named because it leads the entire choir of trumpeters with its principal or main notes. 92

Tonguing

The German and [other highly] trained trumpeters have great superiority over everyone else, especially in the playing of these field pieces, because they make use hereby of certain ornaments (*Manieren*) and special skills (*Vortheile*), through which field piece and principale playing is very much embellished and improved. These [embellishments and skills] are called tonguing, or the stroke of the tongue, and huffing (*Haue*).

The first is so designated because one cannot perform it other than with a certain stroke and thrust of the tongue, by means of pronouncing certain short syllables into the mouthpiece. This tongue stroke is of different kinds, for both in single and in double tonguing one does not pronounce the syllables in one manner only.[43]

---

1   That the clarino players like to sustain the high tones c''', d''', and e''', is, to be sure, a good custom.

43   This is one of the most important characteristics of Baroque tonguing, at least in Germany; and it is opposed to our present-day emphasis on equality of tonguing on every note. See also Altenburg's remark at the top of p. 97, under no. 3, on unequal articulation in clarino playing.

I do not hesitate to reveal this secret because I know that it will not prove to be to anyone's detriment.

[The secret] consists namely therein, that in single tonguing one uses only the four syllables **ritiriton** or **kitikiton,** and in double tonguing one prefaces [them with] the syllable **ti**—for example, **tiritiriton** or **tikitikiton.** These syllables or tonguings are used only in the low register, and appear in musical notation as follows:

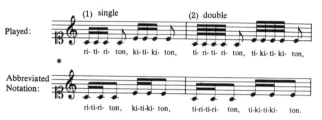

It can be seen that in the performance of these two tonguings there are certainly just as many syllables as there are notes. However, in the interest of brevity, this notation is not necessary. These syllables are sometimes exchanged, depending on the circumstances and the music, so that the last syllable **ton** is expressed first and the others thereafter. An example will make the matter clearer:

It thus depends mainly on the eighth note, whether it comes first or at the end.

Breaking-off of the March

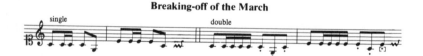

It is true that some have tried to use this tonguing in the high or clarino octave, and I have heard some would-be virtuosos [try it], but I can state with certainty that this kind of exaggerated artificiality is more fantastic than artistic.

Moreover, for the performance of the following passage one certainly needs a [well-]trained and fluent tongue.

---

* Since the principale usually plays in the lower register, its part is generally written in the soprano clef.

Huffing is indeed also of different kinds, but actually, only two kinds [need concern us]. The first can be called the **breaking** *(überschlagende)* [huff], because in its execution two certain tones always break over one another, as it were.

The second is called the **beating** *(schwebende)* [huff] because the note on 94 which it is played is expressed, now loudly, now softly, with a quivering or a beating.[44]

The dots underneath indicate the beating, and the *f* and the *p* [indicate] the different loudness and softness of the tone. As is indicated, one can perform [this huff with] increasing or decreasing [volume].

However, it must be remembered that huffing takes place only at the end in the playing of field pieces or at table, but never, or only rarely, in the middle [of the piece] or in the principale [part].

Nevertheless, the use of the so-called tonguing and huffing is very great and almost indispensable. One will be quickly convinced hereof if one hears a trumpeter to whom these mysteries of the art are not unknown. Since brethren-in-art [have been] in the habit of learning these field pieces merely by ear from one another, and because of the reproach which is to be feared for [having] revealed their secrets,—both these considerations have with reason prevented me from making these [field pieces] known through musical notation.

44 Since both of these kinds of huffing are found in the works of J. S. Bach (in the *Mass in B minor,* for example), particularly at final cadences, we have here in Altenburg's remarks a clear indication as to their execution. In no case are all the notes to be tongued equally. The "beats" in the "beating huff" are probably not tongued at all and have an effect similar to the "beats" perceived in the tuning of keyboard or stringed instruments; hence the German technical expression *Schwebung,* which refers to this kind of beat.

Chapter 11

On Clarino Playing
and the Style of Execution
Required Thereby

In olden times the trumpet, of which we are speaking here, was called *clario, claro,* or *clarasius* [45] in Latin on account of its high, clear tone, [terms] which the French translated as *clairon* and the Italians as *clarino*. [46] It is properly a shorter trumpet, more closely wound than the usual [instrument], and is called a *clarion* by the English.[m] Matteson says that the term **Clarin** particularly befits the trumpet when it is muted. We understand [the terms] *Clarin* or *Clarin part* to have approximately the same meaning as the soprano part *(Discant)* in vocal music: namely, a certain melody which is played mostly in the two-line octave [and which is] thus high and clear. The proper embouchure for the formation of this sound is extraordinarily difficult to attain, and cannot be described accurately with rules. Practice should perform the best service hereby, although much depends also on the structure of the lips, &c. A strong thrust of air and a tight drawing together of the teeth and lips are probably the most important aspects thereof. Regarding this matter one should see [the section in] Chapter Eight on the sound in particular, [see page 70].

He who has attained a particular proficiency at playing tastefully in the

95

---

45   *Clarusius* [*sic*].
46   See the article, "Clarino," by Reine Dahlqvist and the translator, in *Grove's Dictionary of Music and Musicians*, 6th edition. Apparently the Germans used the term *Clarin* before the expression *clarino* became known to the Italians.
m   de Cange, [*Glossarium mediae et infimae latinitatis,*] from William of Malmesbury, *histor. Angli de an. 1101*, Book IV. [The footnote *m* refers to both preceding sentences. William of Malmesbury does not speak of a "clarion," as one might be misled to assume, but in actual fact of *clarasiorum*.]

afore-mentioned high register is usually called a *Clarinist* (clarino player). But one hardly needs to be reminded that a great [many skills] make up good clarino playing, and that the effect is very different depending on whether a musical composition is performed better or not so well.

Theoretical and practical knowledge, and especially a fine, almost inborn feeling for music are also indispensable to the clarino player.

By theory I mean the knowledge of notes, of rests, clefs, signs, and technical terms, and especially of intervals, keys and their various scales, tempos, time signatures, etc. This [theoretical] knowledge is easier to acquire on another instrument than on the somewhat limited trumpet, but it should rightly be possessed already by the aspiring clarino player. It would be very useful for him, particularly with respect to the accuracy in hitting the notes, if he could previously have [had] some instruction in singing.

By practical knowledge for a clarino player, I mean that proficiency by means of which he can perform purely and clearly every musical composition appropriately set for his instrument, according to the intentions of the composer.[47]

Fundamental prerequisites for a clarino player are that he:

(1) Knows how to produce a pure, clear, and pleasant tone.

In addition to the embouchure and the mouthpiece, the player's voice 96 and speech are said to contribute their part towards a good or poor tone. According to this view, one believes that the sound of the instrument will be louder or softer, clearer or huskier, higher or lower, according to the quality of the voice, be it louder or softer, clearer or huskier, higher or lower. Whether or not this view is sufficiently based on experience, we will leave undecided.

(2) Must have the necessary endurance.

For this, strong lips are particularly needed. It is true that they can be [developed] through frequent practice, at least to a certain degree. However, a great deal depends on the structure of the mouth. In order to keep the lips from tiring too quickly, one rubs them with saltpeter pellets or with a lip salve especially prepared thereto.

Some Rules

Every [trumpeter] who wants to play with other instruments must:

(1) Tune his instrument accurately according to the others. The trumpeter

---

47 By "performing clearly," Altenburg is not referring to a clear tone quality, for which he uses the words *rein* (pure) and *hell* (clear) in the following paragraph. Here the word employed is *deutlich;* what is meant is the careful attention to articulation. At this time music was still understood as rhetoric. Altenburg spends no little time discussing articulation on the following pages 96-98.

must therefore carry with him various tuning bits and crooks, in order to tune the two middle C's of his trumpet to the key of the piece according to the chord given beforehand on the piano. However, [the C's on the trumpet] should be a little lower, because the pitch [of the trumpet] becomes higher with playing as the [instrument] gets warmer. Also during the rests which may occur in the middle, &c., of a piece, another tuning bit can or must be inserted as necessary. Lacking a small tuning bit, the trumpeter can certainly wind a small piece of paper around the mouthpiece.

(2) Seek to express well the singing character [48] of the slow movements, and to execute properly the ornaments which occur. Long notes must be sustained with moderation and be skillfully joined to one another. It is well known that the human voice is supposed to serve as the model for all instruments; thus should the clarino player try to imitate it as much as possible, and should seek to bring forth the so-called *cantabile* on his instrument.[49]

97 (3) Make a distinction between principal and passing notes, so that the former are played somewhat louder than the others. In simple meter, the principal notes to which I am referring are ordinarily the first, third, fifth, etc., and the passing notes [are] generally the second, fourth, sixth, etc., which can be played with somewhat less stress, comparatively speaking.[50]

(4) Tongue many passages, whereas others are tied or slurred.[51] To be sure, it is not possible to determine all the cases in which tonguing, slurring, or tying are required. One must seek to learn the proper application of these various aspects of playing by imitating good players and singers, as it were. Meanwhile, I will present a few suggestions.

(a) Ascending and leaping passages, or arpeggio-like sections and triplets with skips can be tongued shortly.

48 *das Singende gut vorzutragen.*
49 This is perhaps the chief precept for all instrumental music from the late Renaissance through the entire Baroque period.
50 This, too, is a hold-over from Renaissance articulation. The best introduction to this subject is Imogene Horsley's article, "Wind Techniques in the Sixteenth and Early Seventeenth Centuries," in *Brass Quarterly* IV (1960), 49-63.
51 *gezogen oder geschleift,* literally "pulled or dragged," whereby *schleifen* had the meaning "to slur" in Altenburg's day.

(b) Rapid passages, and notes following one another stepwise, are usually slurred.

(c) In certain figures only some of the notes are tongued—for ex- 98 ample, the first, or the first two, [or] also perhaps the last— while others are slurred, depending on whether they occur in intervals or stepwise.

However, these rules apply only to those notes over which no dots, dashes, or slur marks appear. [Such notes may] thus be interpreted at the trumpeter's pleasure. Since the high notes, in particular, require a stronger thrust of air than the lower [ones], slurring is thus better applied to descending passages, and tonguing to ascending [ones].

(5) Endeavor to express well a [figure of] emphasis (*emphathic*), which signifies a certain affection (*Affect*) and is supposed to arouse a feeling (*Empfindung*) in the listener. [Such points of] emphasis usually fall on ascending or descending half steps, or when the trumpet cadences in G major. The English are accustomed to indicating it with a small diagonal dash.

(6) Not always play with the same loudness or softness, but rather [in a manner] appropriate to the expression or character [of a] given [movement], and [in the case of vocal music], of its accompanying text. As is well known, there are sundry degrees of loudness and softness in music, [and these] are indicated by certain letters and words, such as:
Forte or *f,* loud, intense; *ff,* still louder; *fff,* very loud; *pf* (*poco forte*), a little loud; *mf* (*mezzo forte*), half, moderately loud; *rf* (*rinforzato*), intensified; *sf* (*sforzando*), played strongly; *p* (*piano*), soft; *pp,* still softer; *ppp,* so soft that it can scarcely be heard, as if it were in the distance.

(7) Differentiate as to where and what he plays. One can play more vigorously when playing with many instruments or in the open air than [when one is] with a small group or in a room, in which case the tone must be moderated more.

(8) There are certain technical terms which indicate the tempo[n] or the motion of a piece, others which indicate its proper character, as to whether it is happy or sad, &c.; and [from these terms one] always [chooses] the required style of execution.

The tempo is indicated by the following technical terms:

(1) *Adagio assai* or [*Adagio*] *di molto,* that is, very slow.
(2) *Largo, adagio, lento,* slow.
(3) *Larghetto, andante, poco andante, andantino,* rather slow.
(4) *Moderato, allegretto, poco allegro, poco vivace, allegro ma non troppo, allegro non molto* or *allegro moderato,* moderate or not too fast.
(5) *Allegro,* brisk; *poco presto,* rather fast; *veloce,* fast; *vivace,* lively.
(6) *Presto,* fast; *prestissimo, presto assai, allegro assai, allegro di molto,* very fast.

The character and [style of] execution are indicated by the following technical terms:

Affettuoso or *con affetto,* moving, with emotion; *amabile, amarevole,* pleasant, lovely.
Brillante, lively, cheerful, shimmering; *brioso, con brio,* lively, boisterous.
Cantabile, singing.
Dolce, gentle, pleasant.
Espressivo, con espressione, expressive.
Furioso, furious; *con fuoco,* with fire.
Grave, serious; *grazioso,* agreeable, charming; *gustoso, con gusto,* with taste.
Innocentemente, innocently.
Lagrimoso, lamentoso, lamenting; *legato,*[52] tied; *lugubre,* sad; *lusingando,* flattering.

n   By "tempo" I do not mean the beat *(Takt)* in the restricted sense of the proper measurement of time, but rather the property [as to] whether the piece should be played slowly or fast.
52 *ligato.*

Maestoso, stately; *mesto,* sad.

Pastorale, pastoral; *piacévole,* agreeable; *pomposo,* splendid.

Risoluto, resolute, bold.

Scherzando, jesting; *sostenuto,* sustained; *spiritoso, con spirito,* spirited, fiery; *staccato,* tongued separately.

Tenero, con tenerezza, tenderly; *tempo giusto,* in the proper tempo; *tranquillamente,* contentedly, calmly.

Vivo, vivace, lively;

... and so on.

Here also belong the technical terms found in individual places: *Crescendo,* increasing [in volume], growing [louder]; *diminuendo, diluendo, smorzando, calando, morendo, perdendo,* decreasing [in volume].

Note. Whoever does not yet have a secure sense of rhythm can count the parts of the measure mentally. For example in 2/4 time count the quarter notes equally, one, two; in 3/4 time and the other triple meters, however, one, two, three; and in common time, one, two, three, four, &c., or count off these parts of the measure with your hand, &c. In slow tempos one should probably count eighth notes for increased security. The most detailed instruction in this and everything concerning the study of time, style, and the like are to be found in Mr. **Türk's** *Clavierschule.* The abridged edition of this is also sufficient for beginners.

Chapter 12

On the Structure and Nature

of Trumpet Pieces

By "trumpet pieces" I mean usually short compositions written for two, three, or more trumpets, with or without kettledrums. One can and must allow oneself a wider range [of pitch] with this category than with the field pieces; hence the melody—and perhaps also one or the other of the middle parts as well—usually lies in the region of the two-line octave.

A proper course in composition cannot, indeed, be expected here; however, it certainly would not be inappropriate to give a few hints on the necessary structure and nature of the [afore-]mentioned pieces, [suggestions] which can be useful at least to the prospective composer [of music] for trumpets.

Above all, I presuppose creative ability for one who wishes to compose. All the rules [in the world] would not be sufficient for one who lacks this [ability].

In addition to creativity, some knowledge of harmony is indispensable, even in composing pieces such as these. Whoever does not yet possess this knowledge must therefore seek to acquire the same from a good method for continuo playing, if oral instruction is not available. Mr. K. **Hiller** in Leipzig writes in the appendix to his *Choralbuch,* p. 24, "In 1791 in Halle the musical director **Türk** had a *Kurze Anweisung zum Generalbassspielen* printed in octavo, a work which I do not hesitate to recommend above all others as [being] concise, clear, basic, even complete. Certain short literary discussions [found herein] on many other musical works give this little book a comprehensiveness far exceeding that of the usual continuo method." I concur completely in this pronouncement.

Since modulation is very limited in musical pieces for trumpets alone, one must therefore attempt to make up for the lack of diversified harmony &c. with a good singing [melody], especially in the main or first clarino part.

The composer for trumpets, [like composers for other instruments,] must not forget that a good flowing melody is the most important requirement of music in general, and therefore also of trumpet pieces of the kind described above.

Next, in writing such short pieces, one must take care that the number 102 of measures always remains the same from one longer or shorter point of repose to the next. It would therefore be faulty to have a phrase *(Satz)* or thought of five measures, &c., follow one of four. In just the same way, [phrases of] three and five measures may not appear in succession. In general and with few exceptions, it is not good to choose phrases consisting of an uneven number of measures—for example, three and three, &c. One should therefore always seek to have pairs of correlated two- or four-measure [phrases] follow one another.

In particular, one must observe whether such musical pieces are intended for short or long trumpets, since one has better endurance and can play higher on the latter than on the former. However, it goes without saying that the composer must have a proper knowledge of the instrument, and may not write such passages as are either completely [unplayable] or [which] can be performed only with the utmost strain and great uncertainty. He must also make provision for the player to recuperate occasionally by inserting rests [here and there]. In pieces of music for several trumpets, [the composer] can accordingly locate the melody sometimes in one part, sometimes in another, just as he must generally be mindful of variety and diversity of figures as much as the necessary unity will permit.

Next, the composer must also avoid the out-of-tune tones named on page 71 as much as possible. At least he should not use them on strong beats and long sustained notes. [The fact] that a very skilled trumpeter can possibly play every note in tune still does not entitle the composer to allow himself [to use] the [above-]mentioned pitches in pieces of music written [not for one but] for several players.

In order to acquire a general view of the customary style of composition, especially of such small pieces of music, one must note the following: (1) The **first** clarino [53] plays the melody *(modulirt)* and the **second** harmonizes. (2) The **first** clarino [53] sustains, holding long notes, while the **second** descends and leaps. (3) They play *(concertiren)* alternately, mocking each other, as it were, and answering [one another]. (4) They make variations, 103 first with simple notes, which are afterwards artistically embellished *(künstlich figurirt)*. (5) They alternate *forte* and *piano*—that is, in different meters and tempos, like an echo. (6) [Finally,] all the previous possibilities are skillfully blended and combined in many ways, wherefrom, by virtue of

53 Altenburg writes *clarino* in a Germanized form—*Clarine*. This could be the origin, or one of the first written instances, of the use of this term, which one finds today in German-speaking countries as a misnomer for the instrument itself, the natural trumpet. Of course, Altenburg himself still uses it to refer to a register or a part.

the art of permutation, many variations result. These [devices] can be use-
fully applied, especially in the little two-, three-, and four-part pieces—for
example, in minuets, polonaises, anglaises, gavottes, canzonettas, ariettas,
bourées, rondos, cotillons, rigaudons, and the like.

Since there are so many different kinds [of trumpet pieces], I would like
to examine each particular [kind] in its turn, such as:

(1) **Solo.** This is played in the clarino [register]—never alone, [however,]
but together with several [other] instruments. It is called a **solo** for the
reason that the one delivering the principal melody plays it **alone**,
while the others merely accompany.

(2) **Bicinium.** I understand this term to mean a little duet for two trumpets,
usually consisting of two short sections. Since the player[s] sometimes
have to sustain long notes and play in the high register, chamber-
pitched D trumpets are the most comfortable hereto, especially when
they are lowered [in pitch] by [the use of] a tuning bit. Since [in] these
pieces [the melody] is always played *(moduliren)* in a single key, one
must thereby endeavor to include as many variations as possible, as
well as such melodious passages as will not tire the lips too much. For
practice in and of itself, the more difficult pieces of this kind can be
played on shorter trumpets.

Some have even set various two-part canons and fugues for trumpets,
even though they are not especially pleasing to the ear.

104

Little pieces of this kind can be written not only in the key of C, but also
in G minor.[54]

54 Altenburg's *Fuga* is not a composition of his own, but first appears in Biber's
Sonatae tam aris quam aulis servientes (1676), with slightly differing cadences
and not including the E♭, but rather E throughout. It has been published in the
original form as No. 11 in H. I. F. Biber, *Twelve Duets for Two Trumpets*
(The Brass Press, 1970). Not only does this cast a shadow of doubt over the
authorship of the other pieces in Altenburg's treatise, including the famous
Concerto a VII Clarini con Tymp. (pp. 133 ff.), but it also points out the great
continuity in the tradition of trumpet playing from at least the middle to the
late Baroque.

N.B. Although E♭ is not a natural note on the trumpet, it still can serve in the key of G minor as a passing note *(transitus)*.

(3) The **tricinium**, with three trumpets, is just the same as a trio or 106 *Terzett* for other instruments. More learning is required [on the part of the composer] for its construction than for [the writing of] a mere bicinium, because the third part has not only the five low tones, like a blaring principale [part] in a processional fanfare *(Aufzug)*, but also its own melody, which consists mainly of answering *(Concertiren)* and alternating *(Abwechseln)*.

107

(4) The **quatricinium**, with four trumpets, or with only two [trumpets] and two horns, is just like a little quatuor or quartet for other instruments, except that the parts always belong together in two pairs, so to speak, and regularly answer each other.

Allegro moderato

[Clarino I]

[Clarino II]

[Clarino III]

[Clarino IV]

108

The so-called **processional fanfare** usually consists of four parts, which together make up a choir, as: two clarini, a principale, and a pair of kettledrums. When the latter are lacking, its two pitches are usually played on the trumpet, and this part is called **Toquet**.[55] Otherwise the fourth trumpet

55   *Touqet.*

[part] is also called *Toccato.* (See **Albrechtsberger's** *Gründliche Anweisung zur Composition,* page 428.)

At the beginning of the [processional fanfare], (1) a lively theme is required, which can also start possibly with the kettledrums or with the principale. (2) No leaping or difficult parts may occur in the two clarino 109 [parts]. (3) The major triad must be retained in the harmony as much as possible. (4) Either the two clarini or the principale, or even the kettledrums, are accustomed to giving variety with a short solo. (5) The kettledrum and principale [parts] must be so structured that these [instruments] do not always blare and thus drown out both clarino [parts].

If now, lacking kettledrums, one wishes to play three-part processional fanfares, the principale part thereto must be written so that it serves not only as the tenor, but also as the bass at the same time.

There is still another kind of processional fanfare which is in six parts—namely, three clarini, two principali, and kettledrums. These pieces create a beautiful effect, and [they] can be used very successfully if the number of players is sufficient, although they are [quite] rare.

It is customary as well for trumpeters to play a piece, usually in the morning, which they call the Morning Blessing *(Morgensegen),*[56] instead of a bicinium or a processional fanfare. It begins as follows:

For my part, I think that the well-known melody of the morning hymn *Aus meines Herzensgrunde &c.* lies concealed in the middle part. In order that it can penetrate all the better, the trumpet which carries the melody of the chorale should [be] played open, while the others are muted.

"Aus meines Herzensgrunde"

110

---

56 *Morgenseegen* [sic].

Kettledrums can also be added to this [setting].

111   The following will discuss this matter more clearly. If the second and third clarini are muted and thus raised a whole tone [in pitch], then the first clarino, unmuted, must likewise tune up to [the key of] E♮. It is presupposed [thereby] that the French, or F trumpet, is lowered a half tone [in pitch] with a tuning bit. Perhaps this kind of tuning has been neglected up to now for lack of a shorter F trumpet. Furthermore, other chorale melodie[s] could also similarly be woven into such a piece of music intended as a morning blessing.

The **table sonata** should properly be sounded at the table of high gentry. It generally consists of eight or nine parts, divided into two choirs, which alternate with one another, whereby one or two clarino players play a solo accompanied by the others. Like other concertos, it is usually divided into three separate movements of which each has its own tempo and its individual time signature. Unfortunately one hears such a **table sonata** played only rarely.[57]

The **trumpet concerto**, which is played by skilled trumpeters, has the same structure as other concertos—for example, [those] for flute and the like—and therefore needs no further description. If such a concerto is set for two solo trumpets, it is called a double concerto. What has to be observed thereby is found in the chapter on clarino playing. It is true that some connoisseurs of this instrument have set trumpet concertos in various keys, for example F and G major, E and G minor; however, these [settings] could not be made in a natural manner without many limitations.

The discovery that on the horn several tones can be produced by artifice which the instrument does not sound by nature has made me wonder whether Art could not also be made to serve Nature on the trumpet. Convinced that [striving toward] the perfection of so limited an instrument must be of consequence not only to trumpeters but also to composers, I communicate the following conjecture to connoisseurs [of the trumpet, a surmise] which I recommend for their closer examination.

57   The *Concerto a VII Clarini con Tymp.* included at the end of Altenburg's treatise and mentioned in footnote 54 almost exactly fits his description of the table sonata and thus was certainly played at table. It is in eight parts—two choirs of three trumpets each, plus the soloist and the kettledrummer—and has three movements.

Perhaps still more tones could be produced if one were to make a little 112 opening on one side of the trumpet underneath, and were to cover it with a key, as [is done] with other wind instruments. **Mizler** has already written that such a trumpet is used by some oriental peoples. I myself once saw a trumpet belonging to the court trumpeter **Schwanitz** in Weimar, on which a' and b' could be sounded perfectly in tune, by means of a little leather slider over the [afore-]mentioned opening. Then only the $d^{['']}$ and $f^{['']}$ would [be needed] in order to [produce] the entire diatonic scale in the one-line octave. This [completion of the scale] would unquestionably be a very considerable gain for music.

The possibility of such an increase [in the number of tones playable on the trumpet] seems quite likely to me by the following circumstances, as well. In 1766 it was reported from [St.] Petersburg that a certain **Kölbel** had succeeded, after oft-repeated attempts, in producing all of the half steps on the horn throughout the range of several octaves, by means of some finger or tone holes. He performed on his instrument and was generally acclaimed. It seems to me that this matter is well worthy of a careful investigation.

To be sure, one could also write pieces of music for trumpets of different sizes, as occasionally happens—for example, for trumpets in C, D, E♭, and F—and in this way [one could] easily modulate to different keys. It would be better yet if one could produce [even] more tones on one and the same trumpet, for usually one cannot easily spare six to eight musicians, merely to have the trumpet parts filled. On the other hand, full choirs of trumpets could indeed play together on trumpets in different pitches, for increased variety. However, there are probably very few composers who have written good musical pieces of this kind.

Chapter 13

On Trumpet Ornaments

In music generally—in singing as well as in the playing of instruments—ornaments are nothing other than certain additions to the existing notes, for the sake of embellishment and adornment of the piece. They are sometimes played loudly, sometimes softly, sometimes slowly, and sometimes rapidly; and depending on the circumstances, [they] are either prescribed by the composer himself or supplied by the [performing] musician through his own invention.

Those [ornaments] which the composer expressly dictates and writes out in their exact rhythm are termed **compositional ornaments** *(Setzmanieren),* and those introduced at the discretion of the player, or indicated only by certain symbols, are called **performance ornaments** *(Spielmanieren).* In trumpet playing there are also certain field-piece ornaments, which, however, do not occur in clarino playing.

By the way, I must still point out that composers differ from one another with regard to the use of ornaments. In order to convince oneself of this [difference], one would need only to ask different composers to determine the ornaments for one and the same piece. Most certainly they would differ from one another now and then. In general French [composers] are accustomed to writing down very many ornaments, while the Italian [ones,] on the other hand, add them only sparingly, perhaps entrusting too much to the discretion of the player. Thus musicians of cultivated taste are required to perform Italian pieces of music, so that neither too many nor too few ornaments will be introduced therein. I would therefore advise whoever does not possess sufficient knowledge and truly good taste to refrain from the performance ornaments altogether, and to play, in a suitable manner, only the prescribed compositional ornaments. In general there are extremely few instances in trumpet parts where an ornament is notated in the proper place. In any event, it can be allowed only to the concert trumpeter to beautify the solo passages of an *adagio, &c.,* through well-chosen ornaments, subject to the restrictions following below. In the middle parts, on the other hand, one must eschew completely all unspecified additions, appropriate as they might even seem. 114

I count those performance ornament[s] which contain a good melody and which are not opposed to the basic harmony among the embellishments [which] in any event [are] allowed. As [has] already [been] said, these, too, should be used only sparingly and with great discretion, because a simple melody is often much more beautiful and expressive than one which has been adorned, or rather disfigured, with ornaments.—Since several pages would not be adequate to deal with these discretionary ornaments even very incompletely, I advise everyone who [might] be served thereby to have such ornaments played or written out for several pieces by an experienced musician. Admirable instruction on this subject can be found also in **Quantz's** *Versuch einer Anweisung die Flöte traversiere zu spielen,* in [Leopold] **Mozart's** *Violinschule,* in **Hiller's** *Anweisung zum Gesange,* and especially in **Türk's** *Clavierschule für Lehrer und Lernende, &c.*

All ornaments receive their proper [time] value partly from the notes to which they belong, and partly, too, from the prevailing tempo. This ornament or that one can also be performed differently, according to whether the tempo is fast or slow.

With ornaments, one must principally observe two things: (1) the notation, and (2) the proper execution.

Because the **accent** or the **appoggiatura** *(Vorschlag)* is one of the most common ornaments, I would like to begin with it. It is applied to rising and falling [notes], to [notes] progressing in steps, and to leaping notes. It is usually indicated by small notes which take their value from the following principal note. The proper duration of an appoggiatura varies greatly, depending on the nature of the [afore]mentioned principal note and certain other subsidiary circumstances. Principally one must observe thereby the following three main rules:

(1) If the principal note can be divided into two equal parts, the appoggiatura receives half [of the value] thereof.

115

(2) In front of a dotted note, the appoggiatura receives two parts of the principal note, leaving over only the third part for the latter.

(3) If a shorter [note] of equal pitch is tied to [another] note, the appoggiatura usually receives the full value of the first principal note.

However, these three rules tolerate various exceptions, which in the interest of brevity cannot all be pointed out here. Nonetheless, I would like to single out some very common cases in which the appoggiaturas are played very rapidly, without regard to the following note. This [exception] occurs mainly when several notes, (a) of equal duration, or (b) of equal pitch follow immediately after one another. Furthermore, [such a case may be observed] (c) before skips, (d) before staccato notes, (e) at the beginning of a piece, (f) after rests, and in many other instances.

116

In all these cases, therefore, the appoggiaturas do not receive half of the value of the succeeding principal note, but only a very small part of it. Moreover, not only is every appoggiatura [which is] contained in the above three principal rules played louder than the principal note itself, but [it is] also slurred to [the principal note]. This [manner of playing appoggiaturas] is indicated in the respective lower staves [of my examples] by slur marks.

The **terminations** *(Nachschläge),* which receive their value from the **preceding** (and therefore not from the succeeding) principal note, are also occasionally indicated by small notes; without exception, [they are] played short—that is, fast.

Further instruction on appoggiaturas and terminations can be found in the textbooks mentioned on p. 114.

The **trill**, the best known but also most difficult ornament, is properly a rapid alternation between two adjacent tones. There are two principal [kinds of] trills: (1) the common or long [trill], and (2) the half [trill] or so-called inverted mordent *(Pralltriller)*. The former is indicated by *tr* or ✹ , and when performing it one must take care mainly to see that it is played evenly. Moreover, the trill always has the note a whole or half step above the prescribed note as a so-called auxiliary note *(Hülfsnote)*. Thus if the 117 trill is on D, as in the following example [at] (1), the auxiliary note is E. If time permits, the trill is concluded with the termination noted at (2).

The **inverted mordent** is merely indicated by ✹ , and is performed in the following manner:

The **mordent** is likewise a kind of trill, but [one in which] the player alternates rapidly between the principal note and the [note a] half or whole step immediately **below** it. There are two [kinds] of these, namely, (a) the long and (b) the short mordents. The symbol is similar to the preceding except that a line is drawn through the ↔ or ↔ [to make,] for example, ↔ or ↔ .

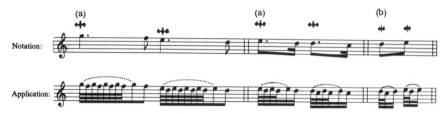

The notes with three beams indicate the value or the required speed only approximately, for ornaments cannot be represented exactly by notes.

118 The **slide** *(Schleifer)* is that ornament in which three or more notes rapidly succeed one another upwards or downwards. For the notation of the slide, one makes use of either a diagonal line between the notes, or else small notes.

That this ornament must always be slurred *(geschleift)* can be deduced from its name.

The **Bebung** or **Schwebung** is properly a continuous increasing and decreasing [of the volume] of a given tone which is sustained according to its value. It is usually indicated by dots with a slur mark over the note.

The **disjunct double appoggiatura** *(Anschlag)* is ordinarily indicated by small notes placed before the principal note.

There are still other ornaments which I will pass over here, however, because they occur rarely or not at all in trumpet [music], and therefore hold no special interest for us.

Chapter 14

On the Requirements and Duties

of Teacher and Pupil

I. On Those of a Teacher

It is required of a teacher that he:

(1) be a good trumpeter, and play the violin as well, because in most cases it is virtually indispensable. [The teacher] should instruct his pupil to a certain extent on the latter instrument also, in order to give him more steadiness in rhythm thereby.

(2) must instruct his pupil **thoroughly**, because nowadays no one, either at court or in the army, is satisfied with [a pupil's] learning merely the field pieces.

(3) must have indulgence and patience with the weakness[es] of his pupil, else he may possibly take away his [pupil's] desire and enthusiasm.

(4) must proceed gradually with [his pupil] from the easy to the more difficult. Everything that may be unknown or vague to the pupil must be explained to him in advance, before he is allowed to play the assigned piece.

120 (5) must also educate the pupil well morally, and teach him how to conduct himself among [his] betters, [his] superiors, and everyone in general. In a word: he must teach his pupil the ways of the world and how to behave properly [in it].

II. On the Requirements and Duties of a Pupil

Aside from obedience to his teacher, which I take for granted, a pupil must:

114

(1) possess a healthy body, a good chest and lungs,° a mouth suitable for a [trumpet] embouchure, firm teeth, and an agile tongue.

(2) possess some knowledge of vocal and instrumental music. Therefore I repeat here that some instruction in singing would also be very beneficial to the trumpeter.

(3) become accustomed, in his own practice, to beating time with his foot or with his hand, as is pointed out on p. 100.

(4) take special care not to play immediately after eating, nor to drink anything cold after playing, for the sake of his health, because both can produce an incurable illness as a consequence.

o To be sure, I have known some trumpeters who have come far in their art despite poor physique, and who have therewith even lived to an advanced age. Nevertheless, one can consider such cases only as exceptions to the rule.

Chapter 15

Some Suggestions
as to How a Teacher
Might
Appropriately Instruct His Pupil

I shall endeavor to set these [suggestions] forth in **nine** lessons, without, however, commending my method as the only good or best possible [one].

121
First Lesson

First of all, the teacher must have a mouthpiece carefully turned out so that it is suitable for the pupil's mouth. Then he should show him how the trumpet should be held, so that it balances at both ends when the mouthpiece is in it. Furthermore [he should] explain to him that the required embouchure is produced by a certain position of the tongue and a tight closing together of the teeth and lips, so that only a small opening is left between them through which, with the help of the tongue, the air is driven into the mouthpiece and further, into the trumpet. The mouthpiece must lie on both lips, more underneath than above them.[58]

However, the lips and cheeks may not be puffed out thereby, because through this [puffing] only a hollow, weak thrust of air would be produced, with which one would not be able to control the different tones; and be-

---

58 Altenburg is therefore advocating placing 1/3 of the mouthpiece over the upper lip and 2/3 over the lower one. Mouthpiece placement has been the subject of heated discussion all through the nineteenth century and up to the present day. As a good pedagogue, however, Altenburg prefaces his statements with the remark that he does not consider his method to be the only possible one.

116

sides, it would be against good manners.[p] Play the five or six low tones
c, g, c', e', g', c'' for the pupil, [then] play them together with him, [then]
have him play them alone until he can produce them fairly well, and then
write them out for him in notation, in order to accustom his eye to written
symbols. I would repeat this lesson several times a day, for about a half
hour, but by no means [would I] hurry the pupil thereby.[q]

Second Lesson

Next impart to him a clear idea of tonguing and huffing, according to the
instruction [given] in Chapter 10. At first play for him only single tonguing
on a certain low tone and see that he expresses correctly and well the
syllables which are to be pronounced into the mouthpiece. Then have him   122
practise this [skill] on higher tones, and after that [have him] make an
attempt with huffing and the various types thereof.

Third Lesson

Now take up the field pieces, and first of all the March, because it is
the easiest. When the pupil can play this fairly well, then teach him also
the other pieces and Blowing at Table. Do not forget hereby to tell him
how many calls and posts each field piece has, and how they follow one
another in order.

Fourth Lesson

Since up to now the playing has been done without [written] music,
merely by ear, now it is time to instruct the pupil in clarino playing from
notation. Field piece playing should therefore be somewhat discontinued,
although it should be occasionally reviewed. Now write out for the pupil the
range of all of the trumpet tones, according to the contents of Chapter 8;

---

p   In this connection, [trumpeters] of old availed themselves of a certain leather
    band which the Romans called *capistrum* and the Greeks *phorbion*. This band
    was usually tied around the mouth so that the cheeks could not be puffed out too
    far or other harm [be] done. See Schöttgen's *Antiq. Lex.* [Here Altenburg is
    confusing the trumpet with the aulos, a double-reed instrument of classical
    antiquity.]
q   When playing, have him always cover his head and gird his waist. If his lips
    become thick, make use of the familiar remedies (p. 96).

explain to him the use of the low tones, as well as of the high and of the out-of-tune ones; and show him how they can be improved. Begin with some chorales such as *Allein Gott in &c.* and *Aus meines Herzens Grunde &c.*, which I consider appropriate for the following reasons: (a) because they are easy and well known, (b) because they are slow, and (c) because many endings or cadences occur in them. When he can play some easy chorales and other pieces, then have him also practise hitting various larger and smaller intervals. In this respect have him begin by sounding something like *c', e', g', c''* after one another; then *c', g', e', c''*; then *c'', e', g', c',* &c. In short, prescribe for him all kinds of skips intermixed with intervals progressing stepwise, and continue this practice for a long time, so that the pupil may gradually attain security in hitting [the notes]. Have him write the short pieces in a special book, and see to it that he acquires a good collection of such pieces. Hereby he will learn to write manuscript neatly and correctly at the same time.

123

Fifth Lesson

At the beginning one should not immediately insist on an excessive high [register], for this comes [only] gradually from long practice. It is enough for now if [the pupil] can reach only *f''* and *g''*. First play the tones for him, and then have him play along, until finally he can carry the second part alone. Also make a choice between the easy and the difficult, impress upon him the difference between *f''* and *f♯''*, and see that the pupil learns to produce all the tones clearly and in tune. If the tone is pushed [so that it sounds] rough and screeching, have him seek a better tone through adjustment of his mouthpiece and of his embouchure. As soon as his lips become thick, have him stop playing. During the period of his apprenticeship he must not practise any other wind instrument and should especially avoid the French transverse flute. Likewise, at the beginning, he may not play on the short trumpet but [only] on a longer [one].[59]

Sixth Lesson

At the beginning the pupil should be given the second part, until he has [acquired] a better high register and can reach approximately high C. Then he [can] practise the first part, while [the teacher] plays the second. Here

59   This is also good advice for those now learning to play the trumpet. A solid technique should first be acquired on a B♭ trumpet before smaller instruments are taken up. This also applies to the valveless Baroque trumpet—which, after all, is what Altenburg is talking about: it is better to start on the Baroque trumpet in C and only later to proceed to the one in D.

is the best opportunity to introduce and explain to him gradually the most necessary aspects of clarino playing.

Seventh Lesson

The first year, one should set aside one day out of every week, [and in] the second year, one day out of every fourteen days or three weeks, for reviewing what has been done previously, so that the pupil may exercise his memory and not forget what has already been learned.

The morning should be chosen for clarino playing, and the afternoon for field-piece playing. This method has its good reasons in respect to the embouchure, &c.

Eighth Lesson

One should urge the pupil to play principale [parts] as well [as clarino parts] and should not forget thereby to take up tricinia and quatricinia and other similar trumpet pieces in several parts. It will be very useful for the 124 pupil if the teacher can find a third or a fourth player or even more now and then to play along, for thereby [the pupil] attains more rhythmic security and learns to play together with others.

Ninth Lesson

The remaining time with the pupil should be devoted to trumpet concertos and concertante works *(Sinfonien)* with two trumpets.

Here, for lack of other instruments, the teacher can indeed play the first violin [part] alone [on the violin] and have the pupil play along with it [on the trumpet], so that he can thereby be taught the exact tuning up and the changes [in tuning] of the trumpet, as well as the proper tempo, the beat, the execution, the ornaments, and the like. However in other respects, it is more advantageous [to the pupil] to play with a complete ensemble, provided that everything has been discussed and properly explained to him beforehand.

According to this particular plan [of study], one can spend one or several months on each lesson, during which time the teacher must allow himself to spare no pains to point out his pupil's progress, as well as to improve upon his deficiencies and mistakes.

If the teacher has instructed his pupil in this manner, he has done his duty and can hope to gain honor with him.

Chapter 16

On the Kettledrums

Kettledrums are commonly thought to be far older than trumpets. However, this [supposition] cannot be confirmed with certainty, just as the form of the first kettledrums also cannot be determined.

Form and Nature

The Hebrews had a kettledrum named *toph,* which was in use in the time of **David** and **Solomon**. It had the shape of a small canoe, was covered with a skin, and was beaten with a beater *(Klöppel)* or with an iron rod.[r, s] They are supposed to have named their kettledrums [t] after this very toph, [an onomotopoeic word] which actually means a "sound" or "tone."

Later on, kettledrums were made in different shapes by the Orientals. Thus there were in use among them small hand kettledrums provided with a handle or hand-hold, so they could be grasped all the better with the left hand and beaten with the right. **Francisci** writes [u] that such [instruments] were in use, and that musicians would sing to them, for the table music of the Persian kings. The Turks are still said to have such kettledrums in their armies.

r See Eduard Leig., p. 176.
s See Printz, *musik. Historie,* Chapter 3, § 11, where a picture of [this instrument] can be seen.
t See Dr. Geyer, on Psalm 68:25. [NB. Altenburg refers to verse 26, which in Luther's translation corresponds to verse 25 of the King James version.]
u See [the passage] in his *Sittenspiegel* on p. 1319.

I will not mention anything here about the very large military kettle-drums, since this type of kettledrum hardly, or perhaps not at all, deserves the name of a musical instrument.

A small kettledrum is used by the Migrenian nobility on their eagle or 126
falcon hunt. As soon as they enter the forest, they usually beat loudly on [the drum] to make the eagles fly, so that they can shoot them. The **Indian kettledrums** are supposed to be one ell long, narrow [in width], [and] look something like a small cask, which is hung around one's neck by a thong and is beaten on both sides with the hands. The **Abyssinian kettledrums** are [made] of copper, and are covered on one side with leather. In America, too, with the **Virginians**, kettledrums are not entirely unknown.

Finally there is another instrument, called **Trombe**, which nearly re-sembles a box with a bunghole.[60] (It is 1¾ ells long and has a round hole on top in the middle.) A strong contra-G bass string is stretched over it, secured by a screw, and mounted on a bridge. This string is tuned to [both] C and G after the manner of kettledrums, and beaten with wooden sticks. [Thus its sound] is very similar to [that of] muffled military kettledrums.

Former Use

We find various pieces of information on the ancient use of these per-cussion instruments. Both men and women played them. Among the men there were, in particular, the **Prophets**[v] and the **Israelites**,[w] as well as **Simeon**;[x] among the women, it was **Miriam**, Aaron's sister, above all, who used them just after the fall of the Egyptians.[y] Kettledrums were already used in the [very] earliest music, which was destined for the praise and honor of God.

Kettledrums are used chiefly on the following occasions: (1) on feast days;[z] (2) after the victory, as Jephtha's daughter [used it] as she went to-wards her father;[a] (3) on all kinds of convocations and at banquets;[b] (4) 127
at dances, where they were played antiphonally, [the dancers standing] in rows;[c] (5) for the praise of God.[d]

---

60 *zugespündete Lade,* literally: "bunged box or drawer."
v I Samuel 10:5.
w Psalm 149:3.
x I Maccabees 13:5.
y Exodus 15:20. [Altenburg omitted the chapter number.]
z Psalm 150:4. [Altenburg erroneously quotes Psalm 28:26.]
a Judges 11:34, I Samuel 18:6. [Only the first reference is to Jephtha's daughter. The passage from Samuel speaks of the women coming out of all the cities of Israel with tabrets to meet King Saul.]
b Isaiah 5:12, Amos 6:5.
c Job 21:12, Psalm 149:3. [Altenburg also erroneously cites Psalm 22:8.]
d II Samuel 6:5, Psalm 81:3.

Later they were introduced by the heathen peoples,[e] especially for their feast of Bacchus, on which [occasion] kettledrums together with shawms, horns, and cymbals [were played].

A depiction of this heathen feast of Bacchus is still to be found on various old paintings and coins. [The procession is led by] a maid holding a kettledrum in [one] hand [and] striking [it with the other], and by two fifers (one of whom blows a curved horn, the other a double pipe).

According to **Ovid's** report, kettledrums were even played together with voices.

Our usual **kettledrums** (Lat. *tympana,* Ital. *timpani*) or **military kettledrums** are in the shape of two large round kettles made of brass, copper, or silver. The opening[s] of these kettles, which are somewhat different in size, are covered with strong parchment skins. [These skins] are fastened all the way around with screws, with which they can be tightened as much as necessary, by means of a tuning key; and [thus they can be] tuned to the trumpets. As is well known, they are beaten with two wooden sticks or beaters.

The larger kettledrum is usually called [the] G [drum], although it is very often tuned to A, &c.; the smaller one is called [the] C [drum] and is also often tuned a tone higher, namely to D. The G of the large kettledrum is the so-called great *G,* and the C of the higher one the small *c.* The larger or G kettledrum, when in use, is customarily placed on the right, the smaller one as a result on the left. If they are to be muffled, as for example on the occasion of mourning, they are covered with a black cloth. This [muffling] can also be done by wrapping the beater or stick heads with leather, cloth, or the like.

Kettledrums are looked upon as a great decoration for [any] regiment. If they have been lost in an encounter, the regiment is not allowed to carry any again, according to the rules of war, until it has acquired another pair by conquest from the enemy.

Present Use

Like trumpets, [kettledrums] are used for various solemnities. The cavalry makes use of them for divine service in the field, in place of bells. To every choir of three—or, as others would have it, six—trumpets belongs a pair of kettledrums, which provide the foundation or the bass to this heroic music. However, they are used primarily by the mounted cavalry wearing breastplates *(Cürassiers)* and by the heavy cavalry, as well as at great courts. Now that trumpets have been introduced, [kettledrums] are also common in many dragoon regiments.

e   Catullus in his *Epithal. Thelid.*

Kaiserlicher Paucker.

Engraving of an Imperial kettledrummer, by Johann Christoph Weigel, c. 1700, from the translator's collection. (Photographic reproduction: University Library, Basel.)

Playing from [written] music is done in processional fanfares, symphonies, in church music, chamber music, and in operas.

Playing without music is called playing a prelude or fantasy, and thus takes place from one's own invention or—as we are used to saying—impromptu playing. In this the Germans in particular distinguish themselves very advantageously above [the players of] other nations. A skillful kettledrummer can, by means of manifold beatings *(Manieren)* and artful strokes, hold his listeners' attention for quite some time. He is able to replace by diverse kinds of beatings whatever these instruments lack with respect to the number of tones [that can be produced thereon]. Kettledrummers usually perform their stroking—now loud, now soft, now slow, now fast—[together] with artful figures, turns, and movements of their bodies. The kettledrums are usually placed a little inwards towards one another, so that the sticks can jump more quickly and better from one kettledrum to another.

129

The Kinds of Beatings[61]

To the [different] kinds of beatings belong the roll *(Wirbel)*, the cut-off *(Abzugsschlag)*, the short roll *(Roulement)*, the single, double, rapid *(gerissene)* and dragging *(tragende)* strokings *(Zunge)*,[62] the double and single cross-stroking *(Kreuzschläge)*, triplets, and so on. All kinds of strokes such as these can better be demonstrated than described. Nevertheless, here is a practical [example] as first given by an anonymous [author] in his "Answer to [the treatise on the use and misuse of kettledrums, printed in the] *Musikalisch[-Wöchentlichen] Nachrichten und Anmerkungen* in the year 1768."

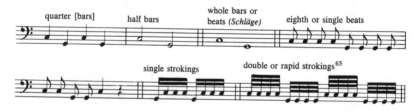

61 *Schlag-Manieren.* NB. These terms cannot all be adequately translated into English since we are dealing with an old, specifically German way of playing for which there is no modern English equivalent, either in the manner of playing or in the resultant terminology. I am very grateful to Jeremy Montagu (London) for his most helpful advice and assistance in the translation of the technical terms dealing with drumming.

62 Because of the hard wooden sticks then in use, Altenburg's strokings could possibly be the equivalent of today's double beating on a side drum, i. e., on the bounce. (My thanks to Jeremy Montagu for this observation.)

63 Does *"Doppelzunge"*—obviously borrowed from trumpet terminology—mean

Processional Fanfare   130

A skillful teacher will know how to use these examples appropriately, instructing his pupils therefrom. It is not possible in this brief [essay] to describe clearly the advantages accruing [to them] from such exercises. As [I have] already said, in this case oral instruction is always best. A [teacher] should not forget to impart to his pupil a sureness of rhythm, in connection with the practising of all kinds of strokings, cross-strokings, and rolls. The kettledrum parts to symphonies and such-like can be used very well for the acquisition of this sureness of rhythm, so primarily necessary for a kettledrummer, since many and diverse rests commonly occur therein. If one has explained everything to the pupil and has showed him the respectively required style of playing as well as the appropriate beatings *(Manieren),* one can, for instance, play the first violin part thereto. It goes without saying that the kettledrums must be muffled for this exercise, so that the pupil will be able to hear the violin and learn to adapt himself to others as far as beat, etc., is concerned. Also, the [teacher] should carefully restrain the pupil from always playing at the same high level of volume. He should rather moderate [the sound] according to the [musical] situation. It is well known that kettledrums [have a] very penetrating [sound] and often drown out the other instruments. One should also diligently emphasize pure tuning, [which is] so important, [a skill] in which pupils frequently are irresponsibly neglected.

I must further note that occasionally, in large musical compositions, four or perhaps even more kettledrums of different sizes are employed, which are thus tuned to different pitches specified by the composer.[f] In order to

>   double strokings or double speed? Jeremy Montagu's guess is speed, and that
>   double strokes were used, as on the side drum, for the roll *(Wirbel).*
> f This is the case, for example, in the conductor Reichardt's splendid cantata of
>   mourning on the death of Frederick the Great.

reach each one conveniently, one generally arranges them in a curve. More-over, a particular fancier of this instrument [once] had a number of kettle-drums [tuned] to the well-known *ut, re, mi, fa, sol, la, si,* and had them
131 placed next to one another, [thus] providing this kettledrum choir with the following motto:

> *Ut re*velet *mi*serum *fa*tum
> *Sol*itosque *la*bores aevi,
> *Si*t dulcis Musica noster amor.

Translation: Let us love sweet music, so that it may lighten wretched fate and the troubles of life.

However, the [above-]mentioned syllables were first borrowed from a great musical reformer, namely **Guido**, born in Arezzo, in the eleventh century. In fact [they can be seen] in the first word of each line of the following hymn, [which was] very well known at that time:

> *Ut* queant laxis   *Re*sonare fibris
> *Mi*ra gestorum   *Fa*muli tuorum
> *Sol*ve polluti   *La*bii reatum,
> Sancte Johannes!

Translation: Let thy servants sing with their whole hearts, that they may let thy wonderful deeds resound, Saint John!

However, since these syllables are actually in use only in singing in-struction,[g] I do not see at all how the above-mentioned anonymous [author] was able to write in his answer: "A kettledrummer [who is to become] truly accomplished shall and must, first of all, go through a two-year period of instruction; there it will then be explained to him what the words (syllables) *ut, re, mi,* &c. signify." This is, however, not necessary at all; in my opinion one can be a good kettledrummer without knowing the meaning of *ut, re, mi, fa,* &c. It also requires not a little time to learn thoroughly the so-called mutation and the proper application of *mi* and *fa.* Of course it can do no harm if a kettledrummer also knows a little bit about the history of music. Because of this [learning] he will still not
132 [necessarily] become a **Martini**, **Marpurg**, **Gerbert**, **Burney**, or **Forkel**, &c.

Kettledrum music is written in the bass clef. Since there are only two tones on the kettledrums, they can also be indicated by a [single] line, for example $\frac{c}{g}$.

[It should be added here] that kettledrummers belong with the trum-peters to one and the same guild and rank, and are included among the

---

g Now and then, the prospective singer, who at the beginning learns to sing the notes alone (without an accompanying text), is [taught to use] the above syllables instead of the letters C, D, E, F, &c. [In this way] he learns to pronounce well all of the five vowels contained therein, when [he is] singing. More instruction herein is to be found in **Tosi's** *Anleitung zur Singkunst,* with explanations and additions by J. S. Agricola.

officers.[64] In some services, where possible, Moors are taken, riding white horses—partly because of their appearance, [and] partly because they are all the more easily recognized [as emissaries] on dispatches [to the enemy].

Fundamental advantages of a kettledrummer are: (1) that he receives double pay, rides his own horse in some services, and for this [reason] in particular receives the [extra] money ration; (2) that at the ransom of prisoners more is paid for a trumpeter or kettledrummer than for a common [soldier]; (3) that he is free from all personal taxes; (4) that a kettledrummer's estate is inherited either by his nearest relatives or by his colleagues, or else it devolves to the local treasury.

A skilled kettledrummer must know how to put his instrument into usable condition again [when it is in need of repair]. According to the observation of the oft-mentioned anonymous [author], when one puts heads on kettledrums, one has to be sure to use good skins of equal quality, to lay the ring around the skin, to put the screws in appropriately, and to tighten them with the tuning key in such a manner that [the heads] maintain their proper resonance.

In the same connection the [anonymous author] advises against softening new skins in spirits before they are put on, or smearing them with garlic, as some advise. Fresh water will perform the same service thereby, and at the same time will be less harmful than those corrosive agents.

[All] this [which I have written] is the most important information that I have to relate about the trumpeters' and kettledrummers' art. I would be extremely pleased if this essay might be received with some approval and [if] some useful knowledge should be found in it.

---

64 *gehören zur Prime Plane*. According to Zedler, *Prima Plane* [*sic*] was a military term designating both commissioned and non-commissioned officers, and distinguishing them from lower staff servants. The upper *Prima Plane* included: captain, lieutenant, cadet (*Fähndrich*), as commissioned officers. The lower *Prima Plane* consisted of non-commissioned officers: warrant officer, sergeant, quartermaster (*Fourier*), captain-of-arms (*Capitaine d'Armes*), and musicians (*Spielleute*). Zedler omitted the trumpeters and kettledrummers from his list, designating as *Spielleute* those unmounted musicians playing fifes and drums for the infantry.

"The Departure"—detail of an engraving from 1737 by Jean Moyreau (1690-1762) after an original painting by Philips Wouwerman (1619-1668)

Appendix

133

Concerto a VII Clarini con Tymp.

Allegro

The second choir takes the repeat

that Altenburg's musical examples, including this concerto, are in the key of D was apparently initiated by Hermann Pietzsch (*Die Trompete,* Leipzig, 1906). F.G.A. Dauverné printed it correctly, in the key of C, on pages xxxii-xxxviii of his remarkable *Méthode pour la trompette* (Paris, 1856).

138 **Andante (Clarino Concer[ta]to tac[et])**

143

March

The march should be played in a moderate tempo, neither too fast nor too slow, more according to the feeling than the absolute note values.

For good reasons I have wished to include only this single example of a field piece. In case a court or regimental trumpet corps should nevertheless demand several field or trumpet pieces in two, three, four or more parts, I volunteer to sell copies of such pieces. I expect the letters, however, [to come] prepaid.

144

Minuetto

Because of lack of space, the trio, to which no trumpets or kettledrums are set anyway, cannot be included.

CRITICAL REVISIONS

The revisions listed below were made by the translator without indication in the text. All page numbers refer to Altenburg's original page numbers. All photographs and illustrations, except Johann Caspar Altenburg's mouthpiece (page 82), have been added by the translator.

Page iii: the first word, "Dedicated", has been added

Page [xi]: the words "to Play" have been added (The same alteration has been made in the contents—page [x].)

Page xiii: comma added between "Polyd." and Virgilius"

Page 13: the corrected version of the chapter title reads as follows: "On the Ancient Usage of the Trumpet, [and] the Dignity and Advantages Which Trumpeters Have Always Enjoyed" (The same alteration has been made in the contents—page [x].)

Page 18: comma added between "Olympus" and "Phrygius"

Page 60: Altenburg writes "Heinchen"—retained unchanged

Page [65]: the words "to Play" have been added (The same alteration has been made in the contents—page [x].)

Page 77n & 80: the variant spellings "Anweisung" and "Anleitung" have been retained unchanged

Page 78: originally this page was numbered "87"

Page 81 (& 82): the heading "The Mouthpiece" has been moved forward two paragraphs so as to follow the chapter title

Page 89: preceding "I. *Boute-selle . . .*" the words "the first call" appeared as a heading—"the first call" has been incorporated into the preceding sentence

Page 106: the last note in bar eleven of the *Polonaise* has been changed from g" to f" (Clar. II); a slur connecting the notes in bars twelve and thirteen has omitted; the appoggiatura preceding the last beat of bar thirteen (Clar. III) has been added; the dot in bar fourteen (Clar. II) has been added

Page 107: the appoggiatura in the final bar of the *Polonaise* (Clar. I) has been added

Page 110: all the *fermatas* in bar seven of "Aus meines Herzensgrunde" have been added

Page 117: Altenburg originally wrote thirty-second notes in the first music example—they have been changed to sixteenth notes

Page 118: in the first music example (top line, bar four), Altenburg wrote the two grace note figure as d" and e"—it has been changed to c" and d"

Page 119: the heading "I. On Those of a Teacher" has been added following the chapter title

Page 121: footnote "q" was originally one sentence earlier in the text

Page 125: the chapter number (in Roman numerals) was origin. y numbered "XV"

Page 131, footnote g: Altenburg writes "*Singkunst*"—retained unchanged

Page 131: the word "*Sol*itosque" has been changed to "*Sol*itosque"

Page 132: originally this page was numbered "123"

Page 133: (*Concerto*) in bar seven (the second ending), the notation of choir I and choir II has been reversed—originally it appeared as if choir I played and choir II rested

Page 139: bar 14 of Andante (Clarino 1, Choir II)—sharp has been added before appoggiatura f"; bar 16 (Principale, Choir I)—the original rhythm for this part was two quarter notes

Page 140: Vivace, bar 18 (solo part) and bar 19 (Clarino 1, Choir I)—sharps added before f"

Page 141: bar 30 (Clarino 2, Choir I) and bar 31 (Clarino 1, Choir I)—flat added before b"; bar 32 (Principale, Choir I)—a quarter note c" has been added to replace a bar of rest; bar 36 (Clarino 2, Choir II)—sharp added before appoggiatura f"

INDEX

Aaron, 5, 121
Abbruch, see trumpet music: breaking-off
Abtrupp, 90
Achaeans, 3, 4, 6
affections (*Affekte*), vii, 17n, 97
Agricola, J. S., 126n
Agricola, Martin, 6
Albrechtsberger, Johann Georg. *Grundliche Anweisung zur Composition*, 105
Alexander the Great, 4n, 20
Allein Gott in der Höh sey Ehr, 73, 118
Altenburg, Court of, 53
Altenburg, Johann Caspar, see trumpet players
Altenburg, Johann Ernst
    letter of assumption, 33
    letter of release, 37
Amos (Old Testament), 121n (6:5)
Anhalt, Court of, 28, 53
Anspach, Court of, 28, 53, 61
Apollo, 4, 5, 20
apprenticeship, vi, 32-42
Aristotle, 17n
"art fifer", 43
articulation, see trumpet: techniques of playing
Athenaens, xiii, 21, 58n
Athens, 4, 4n, 20
Aufzug, see trumpet music: processional fanfare
Augsburg, 22, 30, 59
aulos, 117
Aus meines Herzens Grunde, 105-106, 118

Bacchus, 25
Bach, Johann Sebastian
Baden-Baden, Court of, 53
Baden-Durlach, Court of, 53
Baierus, xiii
Bamberg, Court of, 53
Bartholini, xiii
Bavarian Palatinate, 28
Bayreuth, Court of, 53
Beantwortung der musikalischen Nachrichten und Anmerkungen, xiv, 124, 126, 127
Beck, Leonard, xvii n
bell (of a brass instrument), 5, 13
Bendinelli, Cesare. *Tutta l'arte della trombetta*, vii n, 90n
Berlin, 28, 61
Bernberg, 28
Biber, H.I.F. *Sonatae tam aris quam aulis servientes*, 102n
Bonanni, Filippo. *Gabinetto Armonico*, 14n
bore, 8
Bourrée (J. E. Altenburg?), 103

Brandenburg, Court of, 53
brethren-in-art, vi, xiv, 22, 27-28, 30, 31, 32-43, 47, 48, 52, 53, 54, 60, 63, 93 (see also guilds)
Brunswick, 28, 61
Burgkmair, Hans, xvii n
Buser, Ernst W., 41n, 48n, 81n

Cameradschaft, 27
Cammeraden, 36n
Capistrum, 117n
Cassel, 28, 61
Cavalquet, see Trumpet music, *Le Marche*
cavalryman, 31, 57, 122
Celts, 20
chamber pitch, 12, 12n, 83, 102
Chamber Quartermaster, 29, 31, 34, 52, 62, 63
Charlemagne, 22
choir pitch, 12, 12n, 83
Christian, Duke of Weissenfels, 59, 60, 60n, 61, 62
I Chronicles (Old Testament), 5n (13:8), 18n (16:6)
II Chronicles (Old Testament), 18n (13:12) (13:14)
city piper, 25, 25n, 49, 50, 51
clarinet, 14
clarino, see trumpet registers; trumpet types
closed guild (*Zunft*), 27
Coethen, 28
Collegia musica, 59
Comites buccinatorum, 20-21
Concentus trium vocum, Ecclesiarum usui in Prussia praecipue accomodatus, 59
Concerto a VII Clarini con Tymp. (J. E. Altenburg?), 102n, 106n, 130-137
continuo, 75, 100
cornett, vii, 5, 83n
Corvey on the Weser, 29, 29n
Court Quartermaster, 29, 31, 34, 35, 52, 62, 63
Courtois, Jacques, 66
Cybele, 21, 25
cymbals, 25, 122

Dalla Casa, Girolamo. *Il vero modo di diminur con tutte le sorti di stromenti*, viii n
Darmstadt, 28
Dauverné, F.G.A. 134n
David, 120
Denmark, 42
Dessau, 28
Dicasterium, viii
dispatches to the enemy, 31, 43-45, 127
Doge, 29

141